THE PERSON IN PSYCHOLOGY

John Radford and Richard Kirby

Methuen

First published 1975 by Methuen & Co Ltd
11 New Fetter Lane, London EC4P 4EE
© 1975 John Radford
Printed in Great Britain by
Richard Clay (The Chaucer Press), Ltd,
Bungay, Suffolk
ISBN (hardback) 0 416 83130 3
ISBN (paperback) 0 416 83140 0

We are grateful to Grant McIntyre of Open Books Publishing
Ltd for assistance in the preparation of this series

ESSENTIAL PSYCHOLOGY

General Editor
Peter Herriot

5.98

DI

THE PERSON IN PSYCHOLOGY

ESSENTIAL

PSYCHOLOGY

Contents

Editor's introduction

John Radford and Richard Kirby range widely and speculatively in their discussion of the person. Age-old questions such as the extent to which people *do* differ, the effects of emotion on behaviour, the nature of mystical experience, and the possibility of deliberately changing personality are raised. It is engaging to find that the authors do not even pretend to agree. Indeed, their disagreements, bowdlerized into dialogues, enliven their text still further.

Unit D is a crucial part of *Essential Psychology*. Many who are dissatisfied with our current models of man see the concept of man as an individual and social *person* as the best alternative. This is because it emphasizes the uniqueness of the experience of each individual and also the notion that he acts upon his environment in a purposeful way. The books in this unit all demonstrate how personality theory and research is changing its basic assumptions. Instead of personality being described in terms of forces driving people from within or events manipulating them from without, individuals are now being described as persons each with his own way of construing reality.

Essential Psychology as a whole is designed to reflect the changing structure and function of psychology. The authors are both academics and professionals, and their aim has been to introduce the most important concepts in their areas to beginning students. They have tried to do so clearly, but have not attempted to conceal the fact that concepts that now appear central to their work may soon be peripheral. In other words, they have presented psychology as a developing set of views of man, not as a body of received truth. Readers are not intended to study the whole series in order to 'master the basics'. Rather, since different people may wish to use different theoretical frameworks for their own purposes, the series has been designed so that each title stands on its own. But it is possible that if the reader has read no psychology before, he will enjoy individual books more if he has read the introductions (A1, B1 etc.) to the units to which they belong. Readers of the units concerned with applications of psychology (E, F) may benefit from reading all the introductions.

A word about references in the text to the work of other writers – e.g. 'Smith (1974)'. These occur where the author feels he must acknowledge an important concept or some crucial evidence by name. The book or article referred to will be listed in the bibliography (which doubles as name index) at the back of the book. The reader is invited to consult these sources if he wishes to explore topics further.

We hope you enjoy psychology.

Peter Herriot

1
What is a person?

Explanations and excuses

The first thing we want to explain is our method of joint authorship. First, we discussed the issues involved and made a general collection of relevant material. Then we constructed a fairly detailed outline of each chapter, on which we were agreed. This was circulated to other appropriate authors in the series for comment (of course we didn't intend to take too much notice of the comment). Next RK (mainly) compiled an elaborate dossier of source material and personal comment for each chapter, which JR was supposed to read. JR then cast the joint thoughts, and agreed material, into words. This version was debated until both were satisfied or one was exhausted. Thus, 'we' implies an agreement of the two authors. Where 'I' is used, initials will indicate which of us is addressing you.

The next thing to explain is that even a relatively short book in Psychology depends upon quite a large number of other published works – books and scientific papers. In this series, it is agreed that each book will include only a limited number of references, mainly to guide the reader who wants to learn more. We, in our own writing, have had to compile quite a large bibliography. If there are readers who wish to have a copy, we will do our best to supply one on request to us care of the publishers.

The main excuse we want to make is that, when we started we had the ambitious hope that we might be able to include most of the important material, and even suggest answers to some of the important questions. We now realize we shall be lucky if we can raise the questions, and give at least a guide to the main landmarks. This is partly because there just is a lot, quite a lot of it not strictly in Psychology at all; and partly because of our own deficiencies. Apart from the fact that even together we are far from omniscient, RK thinks that JR is too simple-minded and dogmatic; JR thinks that RK is too mystical and fond of long words.

We forget who said that inside every fat book there is a thin book trying to get out. This thin book – half-starved, even – comes before you all unprotected by layers of padding in many pages. We hope you like it.

The person in psychology

This is an introduction to personality, emotion and motivation. Each of these is treated more fully elsewhere in the series: Phil Evans discusses motivation and emotion in D2; David Peck examines personality theories in his book of that title (D3); we consider individual differences in our other book in the series (D4). Our task here is to introduce some key issues in these areas.

It is natural to ask why personality, emotion, and motivation are spoken of in the same phrase. This is partly the result of an administrative accident: there are many branches of psychological inquiry, and they have to be grouped into manageable blocks. There is also, however, some reason to put these particular three topics together. 'Personality' is used to refer to ways in which people differ (hence the overlap with individual differences) and ways in which they are the same. The study of their common features usually introduces the study of their motives (Freud's theory of 'personality' is a good example of the juxtaposition of 'personality' and 'motivation'). And the connection of motivation and emotion is one which has been debated vigorously for a long time.

We chose our title because our task is to introduce three fields of psychological inquiry. But there is also emerging in Psychology (we don't know whether this will be a permanent movement) a plea for the study of the whole person (Allport, 1961; Bannister and Fransella, 1971; Carlson, 1970; Ruddock, 1972). When these authors speak of 'person' they are referring to a functioning, integrated whole, in which those aspects of personality which are common to all human beings, and those which are unique to a particular individual, integrate to form the motivational system and emotional dispositions of that individual. Thus the concept of 'person', it is hoped, serves to unify the issues treated in this unit. It also reflects a movement in contemporary psychological science. Gordon Allport, in his great introductory text *Pattern and Growth in Personality*, entitled his last chapter *The person in psychology*. He regarded 'the person' as a concept of the future for the psychology of personality – a field which is also sometimes known as personology.

We pick up this hint; and start by asking, what is a person? It is never too early to raise the problem of definitions, one which has caused so much confusion in Psychology. The confusion seems to have been due to the puzzlement of philosophers and the relative isolation of psychologists, who have often proceeded as though philosophy did not exist (see F1, F7). Serious problems have always been posed by apparently non-definable words such as justice or virtue. Psychological terms such as intelligence seemed to fall into

11

this category. Symposia were held on the definition of intelligence; and psychologists were embarrassed by the criticism that they could hardly measure intelligence if they could not agree on what it is. The problem seemed to be one of somehow capturing the real meaning of a word or phrase in another word or phrase. At least two philosophers of genius, Wittgenstein and Popper, have put forward arguments which seem to dissolve the problem of definition.

Three aspects of their solution are particularly relevant to Psychology. First, there is the realization that the 'meaning' of words or phrases – that which we seek in definitions – can be no more than the arbitrarily chosen *usages* which we assign to them. Words and phrases are labels which we use to communicate and to order our universe. Because the referent or denotation of a word is chosen by an act of arbitrary linguistic convention, we must resist the temptation to look for any 'real' meaning beyond this. Secondly, there is the easily overlooked fact that in the course of its public life a word or phrase may acquire a variety of different, mutually exclusive usages or 'meanings' as any dictionary shows. The fact that words seem to have different meanings, contradictory but presumably connected, has caused unnecessary confusion. Thirdly, a distinction must be made between denotative meaning, which is, roughly, what a word points to, or how it is defined in the dictionary; and connotative meaning. The latter is sometimes referred to as the 'penumbra of meaning': the associations a word has for a particular person and the emotions it evokes. Often confusion can be caused by failure to distinguish connotation and denotation. (For example 'intelligence' apart from its limited psychological use, has a host of evaluative overtones.) There is another special aspect of the work of modern philosophers of language. Wittgenstein pointed out that there is a class of words, of which 'games' is a good example, which have 'multi-componential meanings'. That is to say, there is a group of features, of which any game must have some; but such that any two games may have no features in common.

In the light of this approach we hope to avoid embarrassing questions about what a person 'really' is, or what personality 'really' consists of. Words must be our servants and not our masters (the problem that faced Alice when she met Humpty Dumpty). When we ask 'what is a person?' we are not asking about words but about human beings, about their possible distinguishing features, their points of similarity and their dimensions of variation. And our suggestion as to these are not meant as final solutions, but intended for the reader to consider.

Problems for psychology

The existence of individual human beings raises, we argue, two groups of problems for Psychology. The first group we label problems of *individual differences*; the second, problems of *the self*. In practice, the two groups often overlap, but we think it clearer to separate them at least to start with.

But in order to see why there are problems, we must first ask what Psychology is, and what it is trying to do (see A1, F1).

'The study of behaviour and experience' is actually, of course, a whole group of studies. Like every scientific discipline, it is a collection of different problems, different methods, different attempted solutions. Very often these interact with each other, causing general confusion. John Beloff (1973) talks of a 'loosely knit collection of psychological sciences'. Traditionally, experimental psychology has concerned itself with separate processes such as learning, memory, emotions; it has tried to look at characteristics of the individual, usually under the heading 'personality'; it has paid a good deal of attention to the physiological and social aspects of behaviour. It has drawn heavily on statistics and medicine among other disciplines; and to a lesser extent on

13

anthropology, economics, sociology, etc. Since these words in turn are themselves labels for groups of inquiries, another sort of analysis is needed.

Such a one was given by Richard Peters (1953). He pointed out that 'psychologists' have been concerned with four different sorts of questions. These are as follows. First, questions of *theory*: attempts to establish what is the case and always will be the case. Both science and history, as generally understood, are represented here. Why the word 'theory' is used for matters of fact will be explained later. Next there are questions of *technology*. Here we are concerned to bring about some given end, although we may not understand in a 'scientific' sense. Traditional farming was largely a matter of technology: and so are traditional child-rearing and education. Thirdly, there are questions of *policy*: questions about what we *ought* to do, for moral or other reasons. And lastly *philosophical and metaphysical* questions. These include matters such as scientific method, and the general assumptions we make, or models that we adopt, in order to explain the universe and ourselves (see F7).

It is easy to see how questions overlap. Take such an apparently simple psychological problem as: 'Should corporal punishment be abolished?' Surely all we have to do, as psychologists, is find out, by experiment, whether it works. But no. To begin with we lack both the theory and the experiments to get a scientific answer (partly because you can't do such experiments on human beings). Even to find out reliably whether corporal punishment works in practice is next to impossible, so numerous are the variables. And if we did find that out, would that make it right or wrong? That in turn might depend upon what our view of man is: a religious view, a mechanistic one, existential, etc.

Now most textbooks start by defining Psychology, not just as a study, but as a *science*, indicating that it should concentrate on the first sort of inquiry. The word 'theory' was used because Peters adopted a view of science derived from Karl Popper. According to this view (perhaps over-simplified here) the essence of science is to propose best guesses about how things really are. We can never reach the final truth, but we can get progressively closer. We do this by proposing a theory, and then seeing how well it stands up to attempts to disprove it. It is no good looking for evidence that will *support* the theory. To have formulated the theory at all you must have had such evidence; and it is always possible to select more out of the infinite variety of observations we can make about the world. Rather, we must specify what particular bits of evidence would disprove the theory, and then go and see if we can find them. As long as we fail to do so, we can go on holding the theory, as being our best guess. If we find the disproof, the theory must give place to a better one.

A good example (indeed one of those that originally started Popper thinking) is Freud's psychoanalytic theory. One of the tenets of this is that, in broad terms, adult character is largely the outcome of emotional experiences during early childhood. If this were a good Popperian theory, we ought to be able to take two men – say, one very aggressive and the other very meek – and define what sort of childhood each of them must have had. Then we could ask their parents and friends about this (of course it could be done the other way round, starting with children and predicting the outcome). But Freudian theory, it appears, can't or won't do this. First, it is said – quite rightly – that different children will have totally different reactions even to the same situation. And then it is said further that even within one individual, the 'natural' reaction may be repressed; so that the meek man might have an aggression-stimulating childhood, but be repressing his aggression. The point is, not that this is necessarily nonsense; it is pretty clear that people *do* sometimes repress strong emotions. But the theory will not do as a general scientific theory, because one cannot say what would disprove it: every bit of evidence is automatically converted into support. Thus at worst, it is more like magic than science. At best, it is a way of looking at things, which *may* be true.

We wish to suggest that quite a lot of what psychologists (and others) have had to say about persons is of this order.

Popper's views, which for a time came to dominate philosophy of science, are not free from criticism. Two points are these. First, it is held that a theory should be falsifiable. This means that we should be able to show that it does not correspond to the facts. But the supposition that it does not is itself a theory. Thus no theory can be falsifiable, for what appears to be contradictory to the facts might not really be so; we can never be absolutely certain. Second, the range of possible theories must be infinite: each one is simply a speculation about how things might be and there seems no way of limiting such speculation. Even if one theory were proved false, there would be no grounds for preferring another. If there are no grounds for holding a theory true, there are equally none for holding it more likely. Pursuing this further would lead us (as usual) too far afield.

The problem of individuals

It is common to say that every human being is unique. Each of us feels himself to be so, and we all have problems when other people react in ways different to ours. At least since Aristotle, this diversity has been seen as a scientific problem also.

Science – or scientists, perhaps – generally aim first to get some accurate descriptions of their subject matter. This they feel will lead to – or even *be* – an understanding of it. 'Understanding' is a rather vague word, usually based on a subjective feeling that one has grasped the main points of the problem, and has some inkling of the next step. The next steps are usually meant to lead to explanation, and/or prediction, and/or control. Clearly not all sciences do all of these. Astronomers, for example, predict well but do not control their subject matter. A historian might be said to explain but not predict. The meaning of 'prediction' and 'control' is relatively straightforward, but 'explanation' has caused much discussion. A great deal of confusion exists over what it might mean to say that we have 'explained' a person's behaviour. One thing this often means is simply that a particular puzzle is solved. 'Why didn't you come in to work on Friday?' 'I took a day's holiday.' 'Oh, that explains it.'

Science generally hopes to do more than this. Generally we wish either to be able to state some principle or law, under which a variety of phenomena can be grouped; or to be able to list necessary and sufficient conditions – that is, conditions under which an event always happens, and without which it never happens.

Obviously both of these are extremely difficult when dealing with people. In fact in our opinion no-one has yet provided a convincing proof that they are possible. Indeed faced with the baffling complexity of human behaviour, one answer is to give it up as a bad job. We do not want to do that, at least not in Chapter 1. Let us look at the main sorts of attempts that have been made.

One answer might be to say that each individual is, indeed, unique, and that therefore we can only understand, or explain, him or her *as* an individual. This sort of approach was advocated, in various versions, by Gordon W. Allport. The general idea was that the psychologist should get to know as much as he can about the individual and his life history, and on this basis would be able to show how it all made sense, as it were, and even to predict what the person might do next. (We hope this is not an over-simplification.)

This is sometimes called an *idiographic* approach (the study of individual cases), and contrasted with the *nomothetic* method (involving the formation of general laws). At

17

first sight it seems a splendid idea: we want to study individuals; let us do just that. In practice, however, it hardly
makes sense to study an individual in isolation since no-one
exists thus. And *how* is he to be studied? Shall we measure
his IQ, or even his height or weight? Surely these are important facts: but every time we measure, we are intro-
ducing a general law. It only makes sense to say that a man
is six feet tall if we know the heights of other things –
especially other men. Otherwise 'six feet tall' is just a
meaningless noise. And, we suggest, the same thing applies
to *any* judgment, whether we actually measure or not. What
can it mean to say that someone is honest, unless we have a
concept of standards of honesty, derived from other people?
Taken literally, the idiographic approach is nonsense. We
can accept it as a plea not to neglect the individual in our
search for general laws.

These laws have usually been of three kinds (Radford and
Burton, 1974, discuss this further). First, it may be argued
that we cannot account for any one indivdual, but only for
classes or categories of people; rather as insurance firms can
say accurately how many taxi-drivers will have how many
accidents, but not predict any single accident. The next
method is to try to find some *principle* or mechanism that
people have in common. Here Psychology tries to imitate the
physical sciences. Physics, for example, does not deal with
how a particular object falls to the floor, but with the
general principles of weight, mass, gravity, etc. There have
been many attempts to find such principles in behaviour.
Often they have a physiological basis, but others (such as
some learning theories) are purely psychological. The third
approach is to discover some *dimensions* along which people
can be measured. The testing of intelligence is an example.
The essence of a standardized test is that it is meant to be
like a ruler or a thermometer: a means of placing the individual on a scale, so that he can be compared with others.

Unfortunately there are objections to all these. One objection to the first two is that they are reductionist. That is to say, they try to solve the problem by escaping from it; by changing it into something else. It is the behaviour of people in which we are interested. At best, only *part* of an explanation can come by translating behaviour into physiological mechanisms or actuarial statistics. One reason for this is that actions are meaningless out of context. An example used by Peters is signing a cheque. This is quite a different piece of behaviour to writing one's name on a scrap of paper; yet physiologically they are identical. Similarly, one might say, the driver who makes a careless slip due to worry over his child's illness, and the driver who doesn't bother about good driving are surely different, yet statistically the same.

The 'dimensional' approach may be compared to army outfitting. A small number of measurements is taken of each man, and a stock uniform produced which fits at least approximately. Similarly (as H. J. Eysenck has said) if we have measured a man's IQ, his extraversion and his stability (see D3), we have at least an approximate psychological fit. What, we might ask, would correspond to the Savile Row tailor? What he does is different from the stores quartermaster in two ways: he takes many *more* measurements; and he *adjusts* the garment. But notice that it is still only an approximation. All measurement has to work within • limits of tolerance. The cutter may get it right to within half an inch or an eighth of an inch: but he has to stop somewhere. Similarly, we argue, we can never get an *exact* psychological assessment (see A9). There are several other difficulties. One is that the tailor's dimensions – height, chest size, etc. – are, so to speak, given. All men have height, and all we need is a tape measure to save having to drape the cloth over the customer and cut it as he stands there (some couturiers do more or less this). With psychological dimensions, this is not so. They are constructed out of the observations that we happen to make. 'Intelligence' is an abstraction from certain sorts of behaviour that *seem* to be important. Another difficulty is that in any given individual, it *may* be the unique, or very unusual, that is vital. The individual slips through the net of measurement. There are not psychological tests, as far as we know, that would catch the unique behaviour of, let us say, Leonardo da Vinci, Mahatma Gandhi, or Mohammed Ali.

Personality

• The fact that there are problems should not make us despair. Problems such as these have led to the study of what psychologists call personality. By this they mean not so much the sort of dramatic qualities that are implied when we say someone 'has a lot of personality'; rather, the particular combination of qualities that makes up each individual person.

Probably most people, in our society at least, like to think that these qualities make them unique. Each of us feels in some way different from all others, even from those with whom we are in greatest sympathy.

But whether it is justified or not, this conviction is partnered by an equally persistent opposite tendency, and that is the urge to sort *other* people out into groups or categories.

• There is a good deal of experimental evidence about this. For the moment let us ask if we do not, without reflecting, tend to think that the Chinese, or the Jews, or football crowds, or the bosses, are somehow more alike than *we* are, and than our close friends and family are?

Certainly one of the oldest scientific endeavours is the attempt to classify people. As far as we know, science emerged from magic and technology at a specific time and place, at Miletus on the west coast of Asia Minor in the sixth century BC. The pre-Socratic philosophers, whose achievement this was, sought to establish, by observation and argument, the ultimate constituents from which the universe is constructed. Thales, the first of the line, postulated water as the fundamental element. Anaximander named 'the boundless'; Anaximenes, air, and Heraclitus, fire. To Empedocles (?500–430 BC) was due the suggestion that four elements were present: earth, air, fire, and water. As part of the universe, man too is composed of these: and his manifest diversity is explained as due to the varying combinations of the elements in each individual. Hippocrates (c. 460 BC), like Empedocles a physician, developed this into a general theory of health and disease, the famous doctrine of the *humours*. Corresponding to the four elements are four bodily substances, and four qualities which we might term psychological: air/blood/dry; fire/phlegm/hot; water/yellow bile/moist; earth/black bile/cold. Health depended upon a balance of the constituents, disease upon imbalance.

This notion has had many and strange descendants. The concept that a man's personality corresponded to the balance of his 'humours' was further developed by Galen (AD 131–201), and emerged as a sort of generally accepted theory, that of the Four Temperaments. This was what we now call a typology. People were classifiable as Sanguine, Melancholic, Phlegmatic, or Choleric. Through many a derivative writer it found its way into drama in the form of 'humour comedy' in which characters are laughable by reason of their exaggerated personalities, at first the original temperaments, then in debased form mere quirks or oddities. Some attack on or distortion of the stable, rational self is very often the essence of comedy.

While the temperaments now seem merely quaint, we retain an underlying suspicion that personality is a sort of balance of varying qualities. And indeed in the personality theory of H. J. Eysenck, currently one of the most influential, the doctrine of the humours is resurrected in a new form (see D3).

Another literary tradition is that of the description of 'characters' as was done by Theophrastus (c. 370–c. 286 BC)

21

and by La Bruyère (1645–1696). They gave little pen portraits of 'the proud man', 'the honest man', and the like: imaginary persons supposedly dominated by one *trait* as it would now be called.

And a third approach with a long past is the attempt to comprehend the person in terms of the forces supposedly acting within him. The most celebrated version is that of Plato, who likened reason to a charioteer driving the unruly steeds, desire or appetite, and courage or will. Tripartite divisions, loosely related to Plato's, were also proposed by Alexander Bain, perhaps the first British psychologist, and by Freud. Indeed a classification of mental functions into intellect, feeling, and willing has been used by innumerable textbooks and theorists.

Orientations

These three long-lived ways of looking at people constitute one division of contemporary theories, according to whether they deal with types, traits or dynamics. By a *type* we mean, usually, one of a limited set of groups into which people can be sorted. Often there is the supposition that *all* people can be put into one of the groups. A *trait* refers to some relatively prevailing characteristic, of which any given person may have more or less. Generally lists of traits begin with the most common, and have no very clear finishing point, for ultimately a new trait might emerge in just one person. *Dynamic* theories concentrate on the organization of motivational forces thought to underlie behaviour.

There are many other ways in which theories of personality differ from each other. One issue is whether we can divide up personality into constituents at all, so that it becomes a sum of its parts, or whether, on the other hand, personality only makes sense if considered as a functioning whole.

Another question is whether we can best understand personality by analogy with something else. Analogy is a very useful and respectable device in science, often suggesting new insights. In Psychology, it has perhaps been overdone. Thus we have attempted to treat people as if they were like chemical compounds (the British Associationists, such as James Mill, who sought to explain the operation of mind in terms of a few principles of the association of ideas); or like machines (behaviourism; roughly the thesis that behaviour is the only legitimate datum for psychologists); or in terms of physics (the Gestalt school, who tried to use physical concepts such as field theory as psychological explanations); or as if they were computers (modern cognitive psychology has borrowed from computer science many concepts such as the program and the algorithm, which are then supposed to be characteristic of human 'information-processing'). Of course they are none of these things: we must not take the analogy as if it were really true.

This is related to a very prevalent dichotomy, between the biological and the social. The debate often appears to be breaking out into open warfare. On the one side are those who feel that a really scientific approach involves reducing human behaviour to physiological (or other) mechanisms which we share with other species. On the other side it is held that man is essentially a social being, and that all his behaviour and experiences are determined by the forces of society. Psychology, in the middle, seems to be torn apart by these centrifugal forces. There is no real reason, we argue, why human behaviour cannot be understood in its own terms, and not reduced in either direction.

Can we study ourselves?

Since Psychology emerged as a separate discipline, about a century ago, most psychologists have felt quite confident that they can develop a science that studies man in much the same way as a chemist studies chemicals or a geologist rocks. Classical introspectionists like Wilhelm Wundt (1832–1920) were not trying to be subjective: they were trying to observe their own mental experiences as objectively as the astronomer studies stars. John B. Watson (1878–1958) the founder of Behaviourism, made objectivity an article of faith; and this view has more or less dominated ever since.

But it is far from being so simple, as some writers, often of an existentialist persuasion, have pointed out (see F8). There are both logical and psychological difficulties.

In the first place, it is difficult to show that any psychological account of human beings could ever be complete. For each explanation that a psychologist produces is itself a new piece of behaviour, which needs to be explained, and so on for ever. Another way of looking at this is that a psychologist must, ultimately, be a part of his own subject-matter, and looked at from this angle Psychology seems to be trying to lift itself by its own bootstraps. Another important argument is that what Psychology discovers must change the nature of what it is investigating. This could only be avoided by a scientist who worked in absolute secrecy and revealed nothing of his findings. The difficulty is a logical one, but also very practical. For example, the investigation of intelligence cannot but be affected by the ideas that people have about intelligence and about testing: and these obviously come, at least partly, from reported psychological findings. There is a good deal of evidence, further, to suggest that what an investigator expects to find will influence what he actually does find. And although this can be guarded against by experimental procedures, it is far from easy to be certain that it is completely eliminated.

When it comes to studying another person, further complications arise. It might seem common sense to suppose that we can understand another person by analogy with ourselves. We know how we feel when afraid, for example, and thus we understand how someone else feels in a similar case. This will not do, since we can only attach any meaning to the term 'afraid' by knowing what it refers to in others. It seems impossible to start the process of understanding going.

Now it is a general finding in Psychology that it is not possible to know the external world directly and completely. To begin with, our senses are not capable of responding to all possible inputs. We cannot perceive radio waves, for example, nor hear the sounds that bats or dogs can. Even among the physiologically possible, we can only receive a selection. Some kind of filtering mechanism must exist, and just what this is has been the subject of vast amounts of research. But it is not merely a question of filtering. It is a question of what form our internal representation of the environment takes. Clearly it cannot be an exact copy, for the reasons stated (and others). It must be somehow more like a working model. This model is gradually built up and adapted through experience, probably on a basis that is inherited.

Some examples of how such an internal model might work are described by Richard Gregory (1970). Take such a simple action as walking. How is it controlled? It cannot be a matter of each step being triggered off by the sight of the environment and the feel of the ground; that would be far too slow. There must be a walking mechanism which is sensitive to changes in sensory input, but not entirely dependent on them. Similarly with a skill like driving (learnt, rather than innate, as walking is). This control model, as we might term it, is a little like the working representation of the permanent way used in railway signal boxes. This concept takes account of several features of behaviour. One is that behaviour can continue in the momentary absence of sensory input: Gregory's example is blinking or sneezing while driving. The model allows us to carry on behaving even though we do not know exactly what is coming next. On the other hand we may fail to adjust the control in time when the environ-

25

ment actually changes. Then an inappropriate action results (such as a crash due to 'running out of road').

, It is plausible to suppose that similar models control our reactions to other people. We are probably born with tendencies to respond to others, in some rudimentary form. We develop mechanisms of response to categories of people and to individuals. These enable us to carry on behaving with respect to others, even when we get little response. But, as with driving, unless the model is sensitive to change it can lead us astray. Anyone who has made a speech has had the experience of 'losing' his audience. When one makes a category judgment about 'the Irish' or 'Negroes' one is using one 'model' to control responses to numerous individuals. In personal relations, it is very easy to carry on treating another in an inappropriate way. An example might be the parent who treats an adolescent as though the latter were still a child.

On the other hand some people are particularly sensitive to others. Some are professionally good at it; in other cases two people who have, perhaps, lived together for a long period seem particularly 'in tune'. So much so that they seem to know each other in a special way. All these cases can be thought of as having finely adjusted, sensitive models of the other controlling behaviour.

This 'model' concept is not, of course, an explanation, but it does suggest a useful way of looking at our understanding of others.

The self

We must now say something of the second main psychological problem, a particularly tricky one. 'The self' is a notion hard to pin down. Subjectively, we all (presumably) recognize something that is 'ourself': something that makes us distinct from others, and something that is more than any intersection of psychological dimensions.

But just what this something is, has puzzled mankind since records began. In one of the most acute attacks on the problem William James (1890) distinguished four aspects of the self: (a) The material self: the physical body, but also family and possessions; (b) the social self: how we are seen by others; (c) the spiritual self: roughly, our mental life – thoughts, sensations, etc.; (d) the pure Ego: the sense of personal identity. James relied on reading and thinking for his analysis; and we would probably agree that these aspects are all important. For example, it may seem odd at first to count possessions as part of oneself, but the identity many people feel with their car or home is well established, as is the *loss* of identity when deprived of personal possessions in prison or other institutions.

However it is another matter to investigate the self experimentally. Michael Argyle (1969) reduces the distinctions to two: 'I' and 'me'. By 'I' he means the conscious acting agent; by 'me', the person that is reacted to by others. Quite a lot of work has been done to show how these develop and function, though probably less, in amount and in success, than on the problems of 'personality'. The latter have seemed more respectable and more amenable to the methods of science.

Currently there is a revival of interest in the self. This is part of a general trend away from the strict behaviourism which dominated Psychology (not completely, of course) for some forty years. At the present time it is again acceptable to study inner experience. Some psychologists, at least, acknowledge with becoming modesty that the individual in Western civilization is not necessarily the standard against • which all others are to be judged (see C4). We cannot here trace the multifarious causes of this shift. We resist the temptation to think, however, that this is the last word.

Indeed interest in individuality occurs in all sorts of contexts. Modern techniques of government have led us to accepting its demands for proof of identity in the form of computer records and passports, to a degree unheard of seventy years ago. Fiction (e.g. *Cards of Identity* by Nigel Dennis) deals, not altogether lightheartedly, with what it means to be an individual in a mass society.

The theme, however, is an ancient one. As has often been remarked, 'person' comes from 'persona', the mask used in classical drama to indicate a character. What happens when the individual removes his mask was a favourite theme of Molière, yielding comedy but also irony (in *Le Misanthrope*, almost tragedy as Alceste strives desperately to be honest in a world of sham). The mind-blowing humour of an all-out attack on individual identity in the films of the Marx Brothers is brilliantly shown by Allen Eyles, 1966. (Note, just one example, the mirror scene in *Duck Soup*.)

Feeling and willing

Motivation and emotion, as problems for psychological study, are often grouped with personality and the self. This is partly because they just happen to have interested the same investigators. It is also partly because they have not seemed to lend themselves to the same sort of analysis into mechanisms as have learning, perception, memory, etc. And partly, too, because what an individual wants to do, and what he feels, seem more intimately bound up with his personhood than those cognitive processes. None of these reasons really stands up to scrutiny. What one knows, how one perceives the world, are just as much part of oneself as one's ambitions or fears. To some extent, indeed, the concept of 'the self' can be useful in unifying the diverse techniques and data which for convenience we file in different boxes.

On the other hand some of the conceptual problems

28

raised by motivation and emotion are closely linked to those raised by the person. For example, the puzzle of unconscious wishes. Just how are we to understand the assumption, generally accepted since Freud, that we can be driven to do things by desires of which we are unaware? Does it make sense to give such an explanation for all our behaviour? Or on the other hand should we rather say that we 'really' want to do all the things we do, whatever lies beneath?

And to the individual, his strivings and feelings seem, often, to be the unifying force of his life, that which, in a sense, makes him most definitely a person. (Read, for example, *Mein Kampf* or, more pleasurably, the autobiography of Bertrand Russell.)

The individual

If Psychology is to be psychological, and not sociological, biological, mechanical, or what not, it must deal with the problems of the individual. In this text we can touch on some of these, but others will come elsewhere in the series, in particular in the volume on *Individual Differences* (D4).

It can be argued that those achievements of mankind that we most admire are the work of individuals. Of course, working with the equipment of brain and body which is, *very* approximately, common to us all. Of course, working within a particular culture with its manifold and as yet largely unknown effects. But it is the achievement of the individual to transcend the general, and the forces shaping all our lives.

Thus the puzzles raised by the existence of individual persons involve, at the least, all the sorts of inquiry we mentioned earlier; and in doing so, are important not just as intellectual problems, but as central to the function and purpose, if any, of human life.

Wary of definitions for the reasons already explained, we have dodged the issue of what is a person. Often enough, a

29

definition has masqueraded as a theory, or vice versa. Following the example of Aristotle, some one characteristic – reason, or language, or a soul – has been offered as the criterion. Or again, due to some prevailing views about how the world functions, the person has been seen in a particular light which, at the time, seems to provide a convincing explanation of his strange ways. Such were the closed energy system of Freud (D3) and the conditioned reflex machine of Watson; and such too the Christian notion of the imperishable soul, and the Buddhist concept of a sort of onion-like personality, the ultimate end of the individual being oneness with universal being.

It seems to us that the nature of science is such that it is never possible to tell whether our knowledge is much or little. From a purely practical point of view, a good deal more is workably established about the person than a hundred years ago. Persons can be aided or hindered in their development, and plausible views advanced as to why methods work. It would be false to think, however, that we could provide more than an almost childlike answer to a question such as 'why was Hitler the person he was, and Russell the person *he* was?' And when we further consider the vast range of historical variations, to say nothing of human potentialities yet undeveloped, we have, in a well known phrase, a lot to be modest about.

As a basis for some of what we shall say, let us offer the following characteristics of personhood: a sense of identity; the ability to act autonomously or independently; contact with reality.

2
How does the person relate to society?

RK: I'm still very unhappy about Chapter 1. We haven't told the reader what a person is at all; we haven't defined the attributes of personhood.

JR: We haven't told him because we don't know. Nobody does. We've made a few suggestions the reader may like to think about. I am more worried that we are not dealing with solid psychological issues like the nature-nurture controversy, and tests and measurements. Instead we are obviously going to indulge in speculations about society, and little musings about magic and mysticism.

RK: Completely unfair, you know we have experimental evidence lined up as well. And both the issues you mention will come naturally into the text on individual differences – that's their proper place.

JR: Ever optimistic! All right, I can resist anything but temptation. Here goes on society.

Of course we really mean, how do individuals relate to societies? And there are as many answers as there are varieties of each multiplied together. By no means all of these answers have yet been formulated; and of those that have, many have come from anthropologists, sociologists, economists, lawyers, historians, and thinkers of all kinds besides psychologists. Your present authors' knowledge certainly does not extend to all of these fields. Moreover this is a short book, written against a deadline, and out of a limited knowledge. With that, let us glance at what seem to be some of the important issues.

We must distinguish society from culture, community, race, class, nation, country: all refer to somewhat different aspects of social groupings. We have used society as the most all-embracing, referring to the fact that no human beings develop in isolation from others. Tarzan and Mowgli seem to be fantasies only. There are some records of children apparently reared in the wild (feral children) but their real histories and characteristics are impossible to assess.

We certainly know of no human group that lacks culture. Most people would agree that this plus cognition (language and abstract thought) above all differentiate us from the non-human. Culture we will regard as everything acquired by human beings that is not physically inherited (Worsley, 1970). Different social groupings – races, classes, historical period – possess different 'cultures', each a subset of the whole.

Do different cultures produce different personalities? Anecdote suggests they do. We think of well-known figures from, say, the England of Shakespeare and Raleigh, and compare them with contemporaries of Burke and Johnson: the personalities and the period seem all of a piece. The time seems to produce the man. But obviously it might just as well be the other way round; it may be that certain dominant individuals put their impress on a period. Indeed to a large extent we distinguish one cultural epoch from another *by* such individuals. More likely, of course, it is a matter of complex interaction between these and many other influences.

Anecdote is suggestive but unreliable. More systematic

historical and anthropological studies were for long be-devilled by failure to realize the effect of the student's *own* period upon his observations. The eighteenth century saw a long debate as to whether the newly-discovered inhabitants of Australasia were really men or animals. It seemed impossible that any beings so different could be of the same race as ourselves. Alternatively an equally false view idealized such societies into innocent paradises, free from the corruption of civilization. Similarly polite society until nearly the end of the nineteeth century denigrated as vulgar, or even denied the existence of, the rich folk culture of the British Isles. Even today there are those who dismiss as quaint or worthless such traditions as remain to us.

Studying other times and places may be compared to travelling along a winding road. The scenery does not change, but our view of it alters completely. And it is a mistake to think that any one viewpoint is at the end of the road.

Comparisons across cultures, in particular, are fraught with difficulties. We cannot, of course, assume that universal properties or mechanisms exist, since that is what we are trying to discover. And this means that an experimental treatment – even a 'simple' one like an intelligence test – may have quite different implications in two cultures. It may be impossible to equate conditions, or subjects, or procedures (Frijda and Jahoda, 1966).

Partly for these reasons, and partly from lack of interest or awareness, psychologists until recently have unduly neglected cultures other than their own (usually, that of the white United States of America). The notion of the 'modal personality' became popular for a time (it is still featured in many introductory textbooks). It seemed to give a nice neat explanation of how personality develops, and incidentally of what was wrong with Western civilization and how to cure it (Margaret Mead, 1942: *The American Character*).

It seemed possible to describe the typical personality of a

33

group; and this way of talking is still heard – 'the African is a child'; 'your German is...'. While there may be some truth in generalizations, particularly when based on demonstrable facts: we need to beware of stereotypes, a contributory factor in prejudice. A stereotype may be thought of as a kind of mould, into which each new member is fitted. Thus a stereotype of Frenchmen as great lovers implies a tendency to see each new Frenchman in that light. This would be a distortion even if it could be proved that a majority of the French are exceptional in this respect. Thus it is a special case of the 'models' that seem to underlie all perception. It also resembles Piaget's mechanism of *assimilation*, according to which new stimuli are adapted to the existing available mould.

More recently attempts have been made to distinguish the character of nations or similar groups (e.g. Lynn, 1963). David McClelland (1961) has made a number of attempts to relate the characteristics of national and other groups to individual achievement (see D3). He started from the list of twenty 'psychogenic needs' worked out by Henry A. Murray (1938), concentrating on the 'need for achievement' or n Ach for short. McClelland assessed the achievement–related themes to be found in children's books in a number of countries in the period 1925–1950. He then showed that a high n Ach score tended to be followed, when that generation reached adulthood, by a rise in the particular country's prosperity. McClelland held that n Ach is associated with a Protestant ideology, leading parents to stress self-reliance, self-denial, and other good economic virtues. These ideas are already familiar to sociologists and economic historians from the work of Max Weber and R. H. Tawney.

Similarly McClelland studied the lives of successful physical scientists in the USA, and found that they often had certain common characteristics: a tendency to come from 'radical Protestant' homes; interest in masculine, outdoor activities; avoidance of personal relations and complex

34

emotions. This last McClelland related to the amount of family affection received in childhood.

Such studies can easily be shown to be inconclusive. n Ach is a vague concept, based mainly on Murray's intuition. Undoubtedly achievement, and drives toward it, are very different in different cultures and even between different individuals. Nevertheless there are at least interesting hints here which need much more investigation.

Self-image

One such hint is the importance of self-image: roughly, the way we see ourselves, consciously and unconsciously. The self-image can be related to the same 'model' concept we have already met: we operate with models not only of others but of ourself. An important component of this, and perhaps easy to grasp, is the body-image. In order to manoeuvre our way around the world, we have to know whereabouts the parts of our body are. This knowledge is a kind of complex working model which is gradually built up through interactions with the environment. Piaget and others have shown how the infant has to learn that its feet, for example, are part of itself, always in a certain relationship to the rest of its body. The model remains flexible even in adult life: one learns a kind of extended body image in driving a car or wearing a hat. (W. C. Fields made great play with putting his hat on his cane in mistake for his head, another case of an attack on the self being funny.)

Similarly, one has a total self-image which incorporates both physical and psychological characteristics. Presumably the most important interactions for the latter are those with other people. We learn the dimensions, as it were, of ourselves from the reactions of others. This is probably partly why children 'try it on' with parents or teachers, to see how far they can go. G. H. Mead (1863–1931) stressed the complexity of the interaction as the individual presents a slightly different set of behaviours to a series of 'significant others' – those whose behaviour in turn has importance for him. One aspect of maturity seems to consist in the development of a stable and realistic self-image. This is not to say that the mature individual is insensitive to others and treats everyone alike; rather that his view of himself is not at the mercy of every contradictory opinion he meets.

Therapy, indeed, often concentrates on self-image. Psychoanalysis is sometimes described as 'holding a mirror up to the patient'. This is a little misleading, for the analyst does more than merely reflect the patient's behaviour back to him: he tries to show the conflicts thought to underlie it. Other therapists strive for greater neutrality: the most famous name here is that of Carl Rogers. Rogers considers that maladjustment often involves a discrepancy between the image an individual has of himself (phenomenal self) and how he would actually like to be (ideal self). The therapist tries to help the client (a word preferred to 'patient' by Rogerians) to bring the two closer together by a non-evaluative acceptance, based on a genuine relationship and an understanding of the client's view of himself and the world (see D3).

It may well be, of course, that the development of a stable and realistic self-image is impeded by the unfortunately distorted views or behaviour of our significant others. An extreme example might be the sort of Victorian parent savagely described by Samuel Butler in *The Way of all Flesh*, with his impossibly high demands upon his supposedly sinful child. However we really know little of the ultimate effects of such experiences. Cropley (1967) describes an unfortunate child, 'Tom', who was completely dominated by his demanding and energetic mother. A brilliant student, Tom in later life achieved nothing. But as many anecdotes can be found for opposite results. (For example, the childhood of Winston Churchill.)

36

Among others, George Kelly has stressed the importance of an individual's view of himself, for understanding how he behaves. One of Kelly's techniques for getting at this was the self-characterization. The subject or patient is asked to write a description of himself as if written by another person who knew him exceptionally well. The comparison of this with other therapeutic techniques is obvious. It is worth noting, however, that Kelly's theoretical views were based on the analogy of man as a scientist. The general idea was that we are constantly engaged in the task of formulating and testing hypotheses about ourselves, others, and the world in general. This does not seem inconsistent, at least, with the 'model construction' view we have already met several times.

To return to the effects of self-images, while anecdotes can be found for every extreme case, there is some evidence that groups of people of related interests or achievements do see themselves in similar ways. For example MacKinnon (1960) found that highly creative persons tended to think of themselves as responsible, doing valuable work, likely to succeed: a very strong, positive image. This may well, of course, be limited to his United States sample. Many creative persons (George Eliot, for one) are known to have been full of self-doubt. Hudson, who has made extensive studies of gifted young people, concludes that it is the match or fit between a person's sense of himself and his perception of any particular context that determines what feelings and what ability he will display. In some ingenious experiments (1968), he asked boys to do tests of 'creativity' (such as giving as many uses as possible for a milk bottle) *as if* they were someone else – for example a rather conventional scientist or a bohemian artist. The differences were dramatic, almost as though playing another part released a new set of behaviour.

This brings us to the concept of *role*. Sociologists in particular have often made this a key concept in their accounts of how the person relates to society. The general idea is that each individual has a number of 'parts' – for example father, worker, club secretary, etc. – which require different sets of behaviour. Some of these are permanent, some temporary; some very clear-cut, others rather vague; some the individual takes on voluntarily, others are given him. Some roles may be grouped together, and be consistent with each other, but in other cases one is called on to play contradictory roles. This may result in 'role-strain'. While this way of talking does often give us insights into behaviour, it also has implications which may be less helpful. One is that behind the roles there is somewhere the real person who is distinct from them, just as the actor himself is not any of his parts. But it is difficult to see how this person could ever be reached. Another implication is that the part is, so to speak, there ready to take on; whereas in fact each newcomer will to some extent reshape the role. The best analogy would be with *commedia dell'arte* (in which actors had the conventional part and an outline of the plot, but improvised dialogue and business). But even this, perhaps, gives too little weight to interaction and the constructed nature of the self.

Social influence

The expectations associated with roles are certainly one way in which society exerts pressure on the individual. It is often quite difficult to behave inconsistently with one's role – for a priest, say, to be accepted in non-religious social settings. (My – JR's – grandfather used to have a little anecdote about one distinguished man visiting another, both dressed in the shabbiest of clothes. One expressed surprise, to receive the reply: 'Oh, that's all right – nobody knows me. But what about you?' 'Oh, that's all right. Everyone knows me.')

Roles, and much other behaviour, are often enforced by law and custom. Psychologists have tended to say little of these forces, perhaps taking them for granted or thinking them of little psychological interest. In fact they are, rather obviously, a major factor in behaviour. Not only do the origins of laws and customs call for an explanation, but they exert effects beyond themselves. Behaviour that is illegal not only normally becomes rarer, but has quite different psychological connotations. For example, smoking tobacco and marijuana, as actions almost identical, are totally different psychologically, at least partly due to the legal distinction. Of course law, and more so custom, tend to reflect what most people want: but they *also* either perpetuate or change what that is. Right-wing politicians like to assert that you cannot make people good by Act of Parliament. You can, however, proscribe or ordain behaviour, making it, and its accompanying attitudes, unacceptable or acceptable. Laws, even in this relatively democratic country, are not made by the people, but by a few hundred individuals nominated by constituency parties.

Making people 'good' has been the aim of the controllers of many human institutions, from religious reformers through political idealists to humble parents. Religious and ideological organizations provide for many not only rules of conduct but means to achieve a sense of identity. It is most implausible to suppose, as some protesters seem to do, that most people can exist satisfactorily without social institutions. The trick is to develop and maintain such institutions as allow for the growth of individual autonomy, and do not unduly inhibit the testing of reality. The proponents of most institutions do frequently make such claims for their own systems, which can only be judged by results. Evidence, however, is hard to come by. Some have pointed, for example, to the high proportion of distinguished persons whose fathers were Church of England priests, arguing for the favourable influences of a tolerant, civilized, but not over-wealthy milieu. But it would be rash to claim better results than for any other group.

What research there is, however, does have a certain consistency. Coopersmith (1967) for example, found that the development of high self-esteem in children was favoured by a combination of firm, though not severe, insistence on limits to a child's behaviour, together with acceptance of the child's autonomy within those limits. Other writers agree, and stress respect for the child as a person, warm but not smothering affection, a stimulating but not anxiety-creating environment. Danziger (1971) summarizes such generally agreeing reports. He regards personality development as involving a balance between the individual's need to make demands on others and his ability to accept their demands on him.

Similar views may be found with respect to education which, in our society, is the formal means of influencing the normal individual (C5). Our educational system is a very curious beast. To begin with it is very unusual: universal compulsory education is only a century old in this country, and little older anywhere. Most societies, therefore, have got along quite well without it. Yet today no-one seems to think it ironical that the 26th Article of the Universal Declaration of Human Rights (1948) is the right to compulsory education. Then again, it is such a strange hotch-potch of beliefs and practices: relatively few people seem even to have any clear idea of why they are doing what they do, apart from a conviction that education is somehow inherently good, and the aim must be to have more and more of it indefinitely. (I – JR – base this not only on reading but on interviewing students and teachers, applicants for posts, etc.) A few writers, such as John Holt (1967) and Paul Goodman (1960) have questioned these vague but dogmatic assumptions. Of course many thousands of schools and colleges provide most excellent opportunities, from which millions of young people benefit. But it does not

40

follow that our system is the ideal. Very likely there is no such thing: but at least we should be aware of the arbitrary nature of what we do.

Few people will claim that our intellectual or spiritual achievements exceed those of the England of Shakespeare or the Greece of Pericles. Yet in those societies formal education was confined to the few. In classical Greece education began as physical and moral development for the aristocracy; and this remained a strong influence throughout the period of greatness (Beck, 1964).

The individual and society

The relationship of the person to society is, indeed, very closely bound up with law and custom and institutions. But there are other, perhaps more abstract, issues that must at least be mentioned. There are, for example, highly complex legal and moral questions about how much individual freedom a society can tolerate without disintegrating. Almost every variety of answer has been proposed, from the totalitarianism of Plato or communist China to the individualist anarchism of Stirner. Karl Popper among others has sought to show systematically why extremes of control must be wrong (e.g. *The Open Society and its Enemies*, 1945). His general thesis of scientific inquiry proceeding by the unrestricted formulation and attempted disproof of hypotheses does accord well with much of contemporary psychology. (Not only its methods; compare Kelly's model of man as a scientist.)

A different approach to the individual – several different approaches, in fact – have been taken by existentialist writers. Oversimplifying, it is perhaps fair to say that such writers as Marcel, Heidegger, and Sartre have felt that the task of philosophy and the psychology it inevitably generates is to concentrate on the individual's unique experiences rather than on the supposed objective and universal answers that other sciences have sought for. The individual is faced with the problem of his own uniqueness, and his own responsibility. Ultimately, everything we do rests upon our own decision. Personal development consists in accepting this and becoming fully conscious of it. Put like this, existentialist views seem less startlingly original than they have sometimes appeared to be. I for one (JR) am very aware of having probably missed something when in an existentialist writer I seem to find little that was not said more cogently by Freud or the authors of Buddhist scriptures.

However, such writers have had an influence on psychological views of the person, even if only contributing to the general revaluation of the importance of the unique experiences of the individual. This was no doubt necessary during the dominance of American behaviourists; but many British psychologists have felt that it was a principle of which their heroes – such as Sir Frederick Bartlett and Sir Cyril Burt – never lost sight. Men such as these were able to develop an eclectic psychology incorporating both scientific rigour and human values. Of late, writers such as R. D. Laing have urged existentially-inspired views as a new approach to the person and his problems, particularly those labelled 'schizophrenia'. While these may be valuable for their humanity, both theoretically and practically their use seems more limited.

RK: There is a multitude of ways in which the individual can relate to society. We should at least touch on them here.

JR: Such as?

RK: Just take the word 'relate.' It is highly ambiguous here. One obvious and crucial 'relation' is that society confers or withholds the status of personhood – hence all those science fiction stories in which robots try to negotiate their human identity. Then there is the relation in which society suppresses individuality. It is here that I think Colin Wilson's work is important.

JR: I think that Colin Wilson is a bee in your bonnet . . .

RK: In *The Outsider* Wilson illustrated the extent to which the most creative and insightful persons, who may be the spearhead of evolution, are, in virtue of their differences, ostracized or destroyed. Thus society exterminates its most precious manifestation of individuality.

JR: But what evidence is there that the Outsiders are more insightful?

RK: I must refer readers to Wilson's own books for the answer to that. For the moment, I want to raise the question of another form of relation of the individual and society. I mean simply this: Can the individual change society? As far as we can say, it is possible. Philosophers of history such as Hegel and Marx used to assert that the individual was powerless against the inexorable march of events. But Popper, in *The Poverty of Historicism* and elsewhere, has shown the fallacy of such determinism. Individuals can and will change society.

JR: I must have the last word here by saying that I think this alienated, creative Outsider is largely a romantic illusion.

The human and the non-human

Existentialist writers suggest that men are, or ought to be, concerned about their own existence as individuals. Anthropology, the science of man, suggests that they are often concerned about what it is to be human. Clearly each person develops within a context of assumptions about human-ness. This can be seen more clearly if we take a culture other than our own, particularly a 'primitive' or non-literate, not (technologically) advanced one. The 'structuralist' school of anthropology, led by Claude Lévi-Strauss, has presented massively complex analyses of the thought of

43

• such societies, embodied in myth and custom. To reduce the matter to its simplest, the question can be asked, what are cultural practices for? Virtually all people wear clothes, but this cannot be solely for protection since fashion is often out of step with climate, and since some peoples wear little but ornaments. Or cooking. In general, one can live perfectly well on raw food; yet in every society food is cooked, often with great expenditure of trouble. Why should this be so? A simple answer of course is that it tastes better: but quite clearly taste must be governed by culture, since cooking came later on the scene than physiology, and since societies vary widely in what is acceptable.

Animals, on the other hand, do not cook their food. The view of Lévi-Strauss is that this is part of a fundamental human activity, the attempt to differentiate man from nature. Cultural practices are chosen and perpetuated because they are fitted to symbolize this distinction. Men are part of nature, dependent upon nature, and yet must be distinct from it. This relationship can be expressed in any number of symbols – or rather, relationships between symbols. Thus in the case of food there is a natural process: fresh food if left goes rotten or putrid; and a cultural one, changing raw to cooked. These processes are analogous to the relationships found in other fields. For example:

FOOD   raw (changes to) cooked: fresh (changes to) putrid
SOCIETY   culture: nature
RELIGION   profane: sacred
SOUND   silence: noise.

What is being said is that, for example, profane is to sacred as silence is to noise. It is fairly plausible to assert that, until recent times, loud noises like church bells or bull-roarers had religious or ritual connotations. Such relationships are elaborated by Lévi-Strauss in enormous detail. Lest they seem too remote, consider some relationships in more 'advanced' societies.

Many cultures, if not all, have distinguished between themselves and the uncivilized. Sometimes the distinction has become so artificial as to have disastrous results; for example in late nineteenth-century China the ruling aristocrats were quite unable to accept that the uncouth Westerners were more than ineffective savages. More often the distinction seems necessary to group identity. Greeks of the classical period distinguished between themselves and 'barbaroi' – non-Greek.

As society becomes more homogeneous and all-embracing, it continues to require a contrast, and accordingly we have a well-developed 'alternative culture'. Identity, it can be argued, requires contrast, and contrast requires two parties. It is not just that a few strange young people are too lazy to work, or too sincere to assent to the system. In a way each side requires the other. There is no point in being respectable unless you have someone to be respectable against. Indeed unless there were at least degrees of respectability the concept would be meaningless. Anyone who has attended a political demonstration must have noticed the sometimes almost co-operative nature of the conflict between protesters and police. (In Britain this probably tends to be more ritualized than elsewhere.)

Indeed, to indulge a little further in speculation it can be suggested that we have been able to create quite serviceable myths of contrast as much as any 'primitive' society. Quite apart from alternative culture, consider the fascinating themes of the monster and the robot. Why do these unlikely figures persist in films, television and writing? Could it be that we need to define ourselves by contrast with the non-human? More precisely, with the natural but alien, and with the man-made unstoppable force of technology. Isaac Asimov has proposed his 'Three laws of robotics', famous to science fiction fans. They are basically commandments neither to harm human beings nor to allow them to be harmed. Logically nonsense, they assure us that robots cannot harm men.

But we do still have real human beings who differ from us. No good psychological explanation has been offered for the ruthless savagery with which missionaries, politicians, and industrialists have wantonly destroyed the culture and the very lives of those peoples whose differences were such as to classify them 'uncivilized'. Perhaps only now, when it is all but too late for ever, are there a few feeble gleams of a greater humanity.

One plausible argument about persecution is that it may become rife when the normal balance of society is upset. Take witchcraft. Very many societies have this institution, of which one essential feature is that otherwise inexplicable calamities are due to the evil intentions of certain individuals. They do not, however, have the insane campaigns of witch-hunting that Europe suffered in the sixteenth and seventeenth centuries. Macfarlane (1970) among others has shown how this was largely due, not to a sudden outbreak of witchcraft, but to political and economic changes upsetting a relatively balanced society.

Another noticeable feature of persecutions is frequently the amazing courage and persistence of the persecuted. Heretics and Christians alike suffer torture and death rather than renounce their faith. One aspect of this presumably must be the support the beliefs give to the individual's identity: and conversely it is that support that 'thought reform' seeks to destroy (see Chapter 5).

A society successful from the point of view of the person would be something like the successful family of Coopersmith or Danziger (see p. 40). Aristotle defined man as a political animal: that is, an animal, but distinct from other animals by virtue of living in a particular form of society: the *polis* or classical Greek city-state. Among the probably unique features of this institution was, at its best, an effective balance between individual opportunity to attain fame and wealth, and the communal satisfying of needs for artistic and spiritual expression. In contrast our own society regards the latter as extras in which a few odd individuals indulge quite apart from the real business of life.

Another way to put it might be that a balance was struck between *societas* and *communitas*, using these words to mean respectively the relatively formal structure of a culture, and a spontaneous, shared, direct experience. Greek classical drama was supposed to 'purge with pity and terror' according to Aristotle. This begins to have reality if we consider the highly ritualistic nature of the event, the general attendance of the whole population, the psychologically fundamental nature of the theme. Freud named the Oedipus complex advisedly: participation in a dramatic representation of such conflicts might now be called group therapy. (An interesting feature is that actors were, of course, masked: it was the universal psychological issues that were in question, not the individual. This feature survives in our own vestiges of ritual drama such as mummers' plays. 'They mustn't know who I be,' said one old mummer (Brody, 1969).

Such experiences must have had great but incalculable effects on individual development. In other societies, particular groups have sought to create for themselves the conditions of communitas. This is clearly one aspect of 'alternative culture'. Many communes deliberately strive for relationships based upon shared experience and free of imposed rules and roles. They may do so by the use of 'mind-expanding' drugs; music; the procedures of a variety of religions; and/or by the use of psychological exercises and 'games', old and new.

The particular form this takes now is a little novel, but the phenomenon is very old. To go no further back than the thirteenth century, the aim of St Francis was to create just such a communitas, devoid of possessions, power, many material pleasures, and privileges of all kinds (Turner, 1969). Such shared experience and abnegation was some-

47

times symbolized by nakedness. However successful such programmes are, what always happens is that enthusiasm gives way to order, and spontaneity to direction. It is one of the problems the Chinese cultural revolution was designed to solve. Victor Turner distinguishes three forms of communitas, in effect three stages: the existential or spontaneous stage; the normative stage incorporating some fairly stable social system; and the ideological stage corresponding to utopian models of societies based on the first form, but as it were abstract versions of it.

What I (JR) would wish to argue is that while shared spontaneous experience may provide a valuable, perhaps even an essential, basis for individual development, it is not to be equated with it. It is easy to see how the exceptional artificiality of our society leads to a reaction, and to the creation of many varieties of organization in which individuals may 'find themselves'. Shared experiences are real; but not more so than the material world outside. Needs and emotions common to all require expression; but they are not the whole of an individual. Personal development implies a unique adjustment to reality and the making of independent decisions.

Are we all alike?

'Hey, he thinks I look alike' Chico Marx says in *Duck Soup*. The problem of what, if anything, is universal in mankind is unsolved. By evolutionary chance, we are left with only one genus of the family *hominidae*, indeed only one species of the genus *homo*. But we have numerous divisions within that in terms of race and culture, interacting in a way that is at present inextricably complex. Quite clearly some physiological differences occur between groups, but we do not know whether these have implications beyond their mere existence (Baker, 1974). When it comes to psychological differences we are in a worse case, since we do not know what analysis to make. In order to see whether all groups behave alike we must measure something: but how do we know what to measure until we have decided what is important? And importance, presumably, must be related to universality. We might compare dogs, say, on length of leg; but there would be no point in extending this to snakes or fish.

Faced with this dilemma, psychologists have tended to adopt one of several approaches. Perhaps the simplest is to assume that, on the whole the similarities probably outweigh the differences, whatever each of them turn out to be. This is supported to an extent by common sense, and by the relative degree of evolutionary closeness. It is supported too by the anthropological analysis of 'cultural universals'. Murdock (1945) for example, gives a list of some eighty common elements found in all known cultures, ranging from age-grading and athletic sports to weaning and weather control. The main problem with this is that we do not know any way to equate these psychologically. It is true that all cultures possess music, for example: but how different the role it plays in the life of, say, an African Bushman, a medieval monk, and a gentleman of the court of Louis XIV.

A second sort of answer is that we must start somewhere, and it just so happens that systematic Psychology started in a Western culture. Furthermore this is now the dominant culture, and the one associated with every form of material progress, so that it forms an excellent standard. Indeed from a practical point of view what we chiefly wish to know is how individuals will fare in our own culture, wherever they may originate.

A third view is that we have no reason to assume psychological equivalence between cultures, and must start fresh with each one: but this is the problem with which we

49

started. We hope to take it further in our other text in this series.

RK: I think all these answers miss the point. Any measurements must always fail to provide an objective comparison, because any test or measurement can only be a finite sample, whereas the behaviour of people is potentially infinite.

JR: I don't know why you want to bring potential into it. We've quite enough problems as it is with the people we have. I agree that our tests can only sample, and the population of behaviour is infinite in the sense that we don't know how to divide it up. For example given a piece of wood you could say it is 12 inches or 30 centimetres or any other number of units long. The units are arbitrary, but at least we know what 'length' means in some objective sense. We don't know that about intelligence, say, so both the dimensions and the units are arbitrary.

RK: My argument is much more than that. It is that man's basic and distinguishing feature is his capacity to be an infinitely diverse set of states and contents of consciousness. For this reason, all knowledge is potentially available to everyone. And 'all knowledge' includes the capacity to modify oneself. Therefore we are all the same in the sense that we are all omnipotent, *potentially*

JR: That seems to me a string of non-sequiturs. Even if states of consciousness are infinite, whatever that means, why should that imply being all-powerful? I'm sure I couldn't run a mile in four minutes, however conscious I was. And a collection of beings, all omnipotent, seems a contradiction in terms, to say nothing of being terribly boring.

RK: As usual you completely fail to grasp the nature of human potential. I'm really sorry for people like you who miss the meaning and purpose of life. Where do you think the destiny of mankind lies – in a pub, I suppose.

R: If the beer's good mankind could do a lot worse – and often has.

K: Consider just one argument. We are now producing computers cleverer in some ways than ourselves. Our brains produced these and we can use these computers to refine ourselves, to rule out the differences. Our differences are subservient to our shared potential.

R: Well, no doubt we'll go on disagreeing. For the moment, I'll leave it to the reader.

Some of us, at any rate, dislike the idea of uniformity. Perhaps it is mere sentimentality to regret the past, and we should press on towards some kind of ideal world state. Yet, apart from the unattractive nature of the largest existing states, there seems to be a clear loss in the destruction of races and cultures. We lose a pool of genetic variability which cannot be replaced. We lose traditions, knowledge, feelings whose values we cannot estimate. What we like to think of as our greatest achievements of the past seem to have arisen very often in contexts of a mixing, even a clash, of differences.

However this may be, if the human race is so very various at present, is there any sense in which we can talk of a 'normal' person? There are several meanings that can attach to this. One is that of an individual well suited, well adapted, to his environment. This is the sort of argument that Labov (1970), for example, applies to intelligence. Standards are relative, not absolute: an individual can be said to deal more or less successfully with his particular situation. So there would be no absolute normality, but only a typical mode of adaptation, rather like the 'modal personality'. In a sense the extreme of this is a sort of existentialist insistence on the uniqueness of the individual, who can therefore not be said to be normal or abnormal: for each person creates his own environment and there is no

51

way of saying that he is better or worse adapted to it than someone else to his.

Two answers that have been more popular with psychologists are these. The *statistical* answer is that normality can best be considered as being not too far from the average. The limits are arbitrary, but something like two standard deviations from the mean is often suggested (see D4). One can argue that while a man of six foot four is normal, one of seven foot is not: somewhere between must lie a dividing line. Of course it is much harder with psychological variables.

The other answer considers normality in terms of freedom from *defect*. Since we do not know, once again, what is a psychological defect, this is difficult unless you have some strong theoretical assumptions. These are offered by psychoanalysis, so that a normal – or at least healthy – person is one who is free of the complexes that inhibit the lives of most of us. (The view that 'there is something wrong' with most of us is rather popular with those of a missionary turn of mind, religious or otherwise; see *The Occult* by Colin Wilson, 1971.)

As far as discussion goes, it is just a matter of being clear what meaning we have in mind; but the concept of normality raises unresolved issues.

3
Why does the individual act as he does?

This is the 64,000 dollar question, of course. Taken literally, it embraces the whole of Psychology (and much else besides). We shall follow our usual practice of touching superficially on a few of the main psychological aspects, and glancing amateurishly at some of the more exotic.

This way of posing the question implies the sort of answers we are looking for (which we shall not find, however). It suggests an idiographic answer: we have already argued that this, strictly speaking, is not possible (see p. 17). However, we do want to know about individual behaviour as opposed to, or at least in addition to, general behaviour.

It can be suggested that psychologists have sometimes conflated two quesions: Why does a man behave at all? and Why does he do particular things?

Thus much experimental work and theorizing has concentrated on general behaviour. An action is said to have been explained when it is shown to be a case of something that is common or frequent. Some of the best examples come from *instinct* theories such as those of McDougall, Freud, or Jung. The way they proceeded, essentially, was to make some observations of behaviour, and then postulate one or more common principles that seemed to tie their observations into neat bundles. This is indeed a good start to a scientific investigation, but at least two further steps are needed. One is to specify condition statements, so that we know when one principle is supposed to operate and when another; and then the resulting predictions must be tested. Freud once claimed that his theories were tested 'on the couch'. The aim was right, but the practice deficient, since such observations are made by the theorist himself and, not unnaturally, turn out to support the prediction. The wonder is that Freud managed to be as objective as he undoubtedly was.

The other vital step is also generally missing in the older instinct theories: they do not state when and how each instinct operates. Under what conditions, exactly, is the propensity for co-operation dominant over that for aggression (McDougall)? What determines whether an instinct expresses itself directly or through a reaction formation (Freud)? Maslow's hierarchy of needs, according to which needs exist in a hierarchical order of their urgency of satisfaction, presents the same problem. It is one that ethologists such as Lorenz and Tinbergen have tried to solve: analysing, for example, just what characteristics of the situation (sign stimuli) elicit an instinctive reaction. For example the young herring gull opens its beak to a pointed object with a dark spot; the stickleback is incited to mate by a rounded red shape, normally the belly of the female. Hypothetical applications of such mechanisms to human beings have become highly popular, for example in the works of Desmond Morris. It is an example of one of two tendencies Richard Peters (1953) remarked on as characterizing twentieth-century Psychology: to humanize animals and brutalize men.

This notion can be explored at the joke level: for example the way in which human beings rush towards the sea when the summer temperature rises. Or at the popular sociology level: the 'super-releasing' effects of dolls or wide-screen

54

images of film stars. Or at the experimental level: Fantz's demonstrations that young infants automatically smile at any stimulus having a certain degree of resemblance to a human face. But while an animal nature may lie at the root of much human behaviour, it cannot explain it all, or perhaps the most interesting parts.

Instinct theories, as explanations of human behaviour, are more-or-less at the physiological level. Often indeed they postulate supposed physiological mechanisms. Freud, for example, was confident that this would eventually be possible for his theory.

At the other end of this particular spectrum are *sociological* theories. Human behaviour is to be understood insofar as it exemplifies a general sociological principle such as the class struggle.

Such accounts undoubtedly have their uses, perhaps especially in two sorts of cases. The first is when we did not previously know that a piece of behaviour could be thus classified; and the second is when normal behaviour is somehow disrupted. To take examples from Freud once more, it was illuminating to show that such apparently diverse behaviour as dreams, slips of the tongue, and neurotic symptoms, might all be seen as manifestations of the same process. Similarly it can be useful to demonstrate that some activity – say, escaping from reality by the use of drugs – is not just an aberrant oddity of our times, but is found across a whole range of cultures. Or again, that the excessive frenetic energy of an individual is due to over-activity of the thyroid gland.

But for much, and perhaps the most interesting, of human behaviour, such explanations do not satisfy. Even when the basis of behaviour is a very obvious physiological 'instinct', as with, say, eating, or sex, the actual behaviour is largely governed by other factors. First by rules and social practices: as for example the way in which meals, use and preparation of food, are governed by and serve cultural functions. But even given all this, there remains the individual adaptation of behaviour.

One of the most influential of the 'physiological' explanations for many years was that of Clark L. Hull (see D2). Hull did not actually put his theory in terms of real physiology, but in terms of supposed mechanisms operating within the organism between stimulus and response. It was rather like trying to understand the workings of a vending machine without opening it up. By trying the effects of various objects in the coin slot, pressing various buttons, and observing the outcome, one might conclude what *sorts* of mechanisms must exist within.

In preference to instinct, Hull postulated 'drive'. The difference is that instinct usually implies some kind of goal-seeking. Hull, as a good behaviourist, wished to offer a completely mechanical account. E. L. Thorndike's *Law of Effect* (1911) stated that behaviour that was followed by a satisfying state of affairs tended to be 'stamped in': to become a habit. Hull took 'satisfying' to mean reduction of the need associated with each drive. Deprivation of food results in the drive of hunger and the need for eating. Secondly, the drive/need *activates* the habits thus built up, so explaining ongoing behaviour. Hull's formula was that drive times habit strength equals response. (His complete diagram of the supposed mechanism is much more complex; and just before the response end of it he had to insert an 'oscillation' factor to accommodate the tiresome unpredictability of organisms.)

Hull's model was carefully taken apart and shown to be unworkable by R. S. Peters (1958). First, he pointed out that 'drive' is a confused concept. All we really know is that there are a variety of physiological conditions (including different sorts of deprivation) that predispose organisms to be sensitive to specific stimuli and direct behaviour towards them. 'Drive' suggests a sort of engine which is switched on. Next, drive is an inadequate explanation inasmuch as it does not include the external circumstances. Drive times habit strength cannot account for *all* behaviour: one may, for

56

example, go on eating even when full and even if one normally eats little.

More seriously, however, a mechanical, 'causal' explanation can never be sufficient for behaviour. For one thing, to count as behaviour, an action has to have some degree of intelligence or adaptability. A 'response', even, is behaviour occurring in some situation, with at least the possibility of adaptation. That is part of what is meant by 'response'. A billiard ball struck by another does not respond, but a man does. Then again, the concepts of learning and performance imply standards of correctness. Such standards cannot be part of the repertoire of a mechanical system: they come from outside, usually imposed by human decision. Thus a dog gets a trick, or a rat a maze, right because the trainer has so decided. A robot could learn, but only if standards (or rules for establishing standards) were built into the programme so that variation could stop. Otherwise it would go on randomly for ever.

Of course, as Peters stresses, it is not that a mechanical model is never appropriate, but only that it cannot always be so.

The opposite sort of explanation, in a sense, is that of social *rules*. Peters at one point remarks that 'man in society is a chess-player writ large'. By this he meant to convey that much of what we do is based on the fact that we have some aim in view, and some notion of the means – largely conventional – of getting there. It is doubtful if this was meant as a full explanation. Rules in themselves are insufficient. Not only do we have to account for the individual who breaks or ignores the rules; but we feel impelled to ask further questions about the origin and persistence of the rules. This applies both to the rules and to the individual who follows them.

If one takes such a simple action as putting on a suit and collar and tie each working day, it is clear that talk of drive times habit strength is footling; but social rules will not do either: I am not compelled to do this.

What sort of answer do we want?

RK: This is one of your typically confusing questions. Who is 'we'? Do you mean psychologists, or the general public, or you and I or (as I suspect) just you?

JR: I suppose I only want an excuse to mention the problem that all sorts of different answers have been given, and accepted, to questions about why people do things.

RK: Quite. But we – you and I – must explain here that people calling themselves psychologists have classified their answers under the heading of 'motivation' theories. The reader wants to know the connexion between the psychology of motivation and the title of this chapter. The connexion is that psychologists allocate questions about the causes of behaviour to 'motivation', and have devised many 'theories' to contain their answers. I suspect that these divisions of subject matter, though necessary, are pernicious: the area becomes autonomous and a problem in itself. Hence instead of studying problems about the causes of behaviour we study 'motivation'. But however that may be, our task now is to give the reader a systematic introduction to these theories.

JR: You know as well as I do there isn't time for that. We'd better refer the reader to the volume on motivation in this series (D2), or to K. B. Madsen's book *Theories of Motivation*.

Having done so, one thing that Madsen (1961) points out is that most if not all psychological theories of motivation are at the stage of description and classification. They have not proceeded to the formulation of axioms, to expressing themselves in symbols, or to construction of metatheory (an explicit formulation of the presuppositions of the theory). It is far from clear, however, that psychological theories can ever do these things: the most ambitious attempts so far have probably been those of Hull and Lewin, both of which at present are regarded mainly as historical curiosities.

In contrast to formal theories, what 'we' want is often some selection of necessary or sufficient conditions. By a necessary condition, we mean something in the absence of which an effect never occurs: oxygen is a necessary condition of fire. A sufficient condition is such that, whenever it occurs, the effect occurs. Rain is a sufficient condition for the streets being wet.

When it comes to behaviour there are of course many necessary conditions, such as being alive, having a functioning body, etc., but these are not usually what we are after. When we do go after them we seldom find them. For example the notion of selection by psychological testing is based on an assumption about necessary conditions: that, say, an IQ of 110 is a necessary condition for success at grammar school. (It is usually moderated in the form 'likely to succeed'.) Sufficient conditions are likewise elusive. What sufficient condition(s) can we state for ambition or aggression? The implication of popular psychology is often that such a condition has been found, such as broken homes for delinquency. But of course from both stable and unstable homes come both law-breakers and the law-abiding. The most that can usually be said is that there is a relationship: a correlation.

To get further, we need either a statement of the conditions governing a general principle, or of the mechanisms at work. One of the few attempts to do both is found in the work of H. J. Eysenck (b. 1916) (see D3).

This theory brings together several lines of research, by Eysenck himself and others. One line stems from Pavlov (1849–1936). Pavlov's famous experiments on what is now called *classical conditioning* (see A3), in which a neutral stimulus such as a bell was paired with a stimulus that naturally evoked a response, such as food and salivation respectively, were designed not to elicit the rather obvious fact that eventually the animal will salivate to the bell: they were intended to investigate the working of the nervous system. One of Pavlov's conclusions was that whenever stimuli are paired in this way, a 'connection-forming process', called excitation, occurs in the cortex. Excitation, however, is always accompanied by inhibition, a fatigue-like process that works against the passage of neural impulses. Furthermore, the tendency towards excitation and inhibition varied as between individuals, due to innate differences in the cortex. Some dogs formed conditioned responses quickly, and retained them well; others the opposite. Pavlov's dogs also showed varied reactions to other experimental conditions, so much so that he was able to classify them into different 'personality types'. These types, curiously enough, turned out to be by no means inconsistent with the ancient theory of humours mentioned in Chapter 1.

Another source of Eysenck's theory was the personality typology of Jung. Working somewhat intuitively from observation of individuals, mostly patients, Jung held that people can be divided into those predominantly 'extraverted' and those predominantly 'introverted'. Eysenck more systematically applied the techniques of factor analysis to a large number of measures of behaviour (very roughly, factor analysis tells us which measurements 'go together' and thus are probably united by some common factor). What emerged was not two separate types of people, but a dimension of extraversion-introversion along which individuals are placed.

Extraversion involves a number of characteristics, including a greater liking for sensory stimulation, a more marked response to alcohol, a greater disregard for social custom and taboos. At the extreme end of the extrovert scale Eysenck would place the psychopathic personality, one which seems quite careless of moral scruples, reckless of the future and of harm to others or himself. Pre-frontal leucotomy tends to increase extraversion. It seemed plausible to suppose that extraversion was related to slow or weak conditioning: in a sense the extreme extravert fails to learn social behaviour through conditioning. (The extreme introvert, of course, learns too well, and is characterized by social inhibition and anxiety.) Experiments in which subjects assessed by their behaviour as extravert or introvert form conditioned responses do lend support to this theory (but see D3).

Eysenck has been able to extend his account to include social behaviour and attitudes. Thus one of the attractive features is that he has produced a theory consistent at all three of the levels with which Psychology must deal: physioligical, individual, and social. Hardly any other theory has done this since Thomas Hobbes made the distinction in 1651.

Eysenck's theory is perhaps the most systematic attempt so far to tackle problems of the person as they reveal themselves in individual differences. He has not really been concerned with the self, nor with other possible defining characteristics of personhood.

Four main concepts

Madsen shows how the many 'theories of motivation' – he lists more than twenty – have varied in all sorts of ways: for example some confine themselves to experiential, others to behavioural phenomena. Some of the theories take the whole person as their unit (the molar theories), others deal in units such as stimuli-response bonds (molecular theories), etc.

Attempts to investigate motivation, however, have tended to cluster around one or more of four main concepts: instinct, homeostasis, evolution, and hedonism.

Instinct we have already met. The concept is a very old one. F. A. Beach (1955) in a famous paper traced its descent from Greek philosophy. 'Instinct' has generally implied the existence of *innate* patterns of behaviour, found in each member of a species and relatively unalterable through experience. There is also the related implication of behaviour starting and continuing in the absence of external stimulation, until some goal is reached. Sometimes instinct is contrasted with intelligent or adaptive behaviour, one being typical of humans. D. O. Hebb (1949) saw the two as opposite ends of a continuum. Other theorists, such as the psychoanalysts and the ethologists, have stressed the *drive* aspect. McDougall's instinct theory allowed for adaptability of human behaviour, as did Freud's. Jung's more extravagant version sought to define some super-releasers of human instincts – the archetypes – analogous to those isolated by careful ethological experiment. As yet, no one has seen how to put many of Jung's ideas to the test.

Homeostasis is the principle of maintaining a steady or balanced state. Likewise an ancient concept, it came to the fore again with the work of W. B. Cannon. He wrote of 'the wisdom of the body' (1933) meaning the mechanisms by which under a normal range of conditions, the internal environment – temperature, blood pressure, etc. – is kept constant (see A2). This can be extended to behaviour, first in the sense that restoration of a physiological norm is clearly the function of some actions: eating or wearing clothes (though as we have stressed there is much more to such behaviour). Then it can be extended to maintaining a hypothetical physiological norm: this is a function of tension reduction in Freud's theory. The next step is to make the norm or balance a purely psychological one. Maintenance of equilibrium is at the heart of Piaget's theory (see C2). We may mention Leon Festinger's concept of the reduction of 'cognitive dissonance' (see B3). Festinger's theory asserts that when any two 'cognitions' are mutually contradictory or 'dissonant', a feeling of displeasure is created which motivates the person to action which will reduce the dissonance. Then it can be said that the balance is a social one that individual behaviour is calculated to keep the society in trim, as it were (not necessarily consciously).

The question arises as to how such norms originate; or to put it another way, how we justify postulating them. Ultimately we must seek evidence. Two examples of relevant evidence are these.

Behaviour whose function is to maintain physiological balance was studied by Richter (1942). He showed many cases of animals automatically regulating their own physiology: for example rats, given free access to water and to a salt solution, drank just the right proportions of each. Richter argued that humans too have such self-regulatory mechanisms, and that children on a 'cafeteria' system, i.e. with a free choice of essential foods, will make the 'right' choices. The mechanisms are delicate, however, and can easily be upset: by a disturbance in the physical mechanism itself, e.g. in the taste system or elsewhere; by non-availability of the right substances; or by the confusing effects of mixed and artificially prepared foods. It is well known, for instance, that far too much sugar is eaten on average. The natural regulatory mechanism has been upset by commercial interests. (A curious and tiresome side effect is that those who have managed to escape from this, and can once more trust their natural inclinations, tend to be regarded as moralistic cranks.)

At the level of social perception, several experiments have shown how the individual establishes a base line of his own experience. Thus asked to judge the heights of other people, tall men consistently underestimated, short men overestimated (Hinckley, 1951). With coloured subjects, the darker rated others as lighter, and vice versa (Marks, 1943). Such evidence was taken by Helson (1953) as the basis for a general theory of Adaptation Level, which attempts to make mathematically based predictions as to behaviour that will result from such base lines, which are to be seen as an attempt to maintain an individual balance of incoming information.

The concept of homeostasis has continued to produce new theorizing, and again two examples will be mentioned. Kurt Lewin (1898–1947) proposed a large-scale view of Psychology in which the individual is to be understood as the centre point of numerous positive and negative forces, dynamically interacting in, normally, a state of fluid balance. Lewin's theory was important for stressing some aspects that can get forgotten, for example, the importance of the present. (Many theories stress the past – e.g. reinforcement – or the future – e.g. goals.) But while it excited many enthusiastic followers, it has not resulted in a large well established body of experiment.

In a somewhat similar way, *cybernetics* seemed for a time to provide a new answer for everything. Cybernetics is the science of control mechanisms, the word being coined by the mathematician, Norbert Wiener, in 1948. Systems can be distinguished according to whether they are self-regulatory or not. Vending machines or electric razors are not: thermostats, homing guided missiles, and living things, are. The latter group have the sort of control mechanisms that are interesting for Psychology, and these incorporate the device of feedback of information. This had long been seen to be a vital part of physiological homeostasis, and perhaps for even longer of psychological. Elsewhere we have mentioned the role of the 'significant other'. James Boswell, admittedly an unusually self-conscious individual, wrote of adjusting his personality by the use of his diary, as a woman her face in a mirror. Cybernetics provided a stimulating new approach, grouping together phenomena that before seemed diverse, and offered the possibility of mathematical exactness in the form of information theory.

We must now mention our third concept, that of *evolution*. Darwin's ideas have of course profoundly influenced thought in many fields, not least the whole of Psychology. We can perhaps point this out specifically in the case of motivation.

There was the general change of view that made man one of the animal kingdom. There was the emphasis on those animal characteristics that led to survival, in particular by contributing to adaptability. There was the impetus to make Psychology a biological study rather than a purely philosophical one (see F7).

More particularly, evolutionary theory fostered the actual study of different species for comparative purposes. (Compare Darwin on emotional expression, Chapter 4.) This, however, also had effects, such as the tendency to extrapolate from animals to men. Another effect was the emphasis on innate or instinctual sources of motivation. And another was that on the unconscious or irrational – animal-like – nature of human behaviour. Then too psychological processes came to be looked at as having some role in adapting to an environment. William James, for example, treated consciousness thus. This was one of the contributory origins of the *functional* psychology that developed in the United States, and from which emerged Behaviorism.

As to *hedonism*, we have again a concept that has been with us in one form or another since classical times. It seems a simple explanation of behaviour to say that men and animals seek pleasure and avoid pain. This is not so. As far as animals are concerned, the obvious difficulty is that our only grounds for saying that pleasure or pain exist are precisely that the animal goes on with the behaviour or ends it. This was the problem met by Thorndike when formulating his Law of Effect. He wanted to say that a response followed by a satisfying state of affairs would become more frequent. But how to say what states of affairs are satisfying? Two general sorts of answers have been offered. One, given by Hull, is that satisfaction arises from reducing the need state associated with a drive. The drives are either those built-in to the organism like those for food or warmth, or secondary drives deriving their force from the primary ones (like money). Apart from the difficulties with drives and needs already mentioned, if this account were sufficient there would be no need to talk of satisfaction: and indeed such a mentalistic concept had no attraction for behaviourists. The other approach was taken by Skinner: essentially that there is no way of telling in advance what is satisfying. Or as he more behaviouristically puts it, reinforcing. Stimuli are discovered to be reinforcing from the fact that they increase the probability of responses.

The claim of Skinner (see A3 and B1) is that all behaviour can be shown to have a pattern of reinforcement leading up to it. When we have analysed the pattern, we have explained the behaviour. So many writers have shot holes in this plan that it seems hardly necessary to do so again (see F7). No-one questions, of course, that some behaviour can be modified by carefully placed reinforcements. This is how animals have been trained for centuries; and experiment has shown how to improve the method so that very reliable and complex behaviour can be induced. For human behaviour at least, however, reinforcement cannot be a necessary condition since there is much – for example language – for which a reinforcement analysis in any simple sense is not possible (see A7). Nor can it be a sufficient condition, since many times behaviour is constantly reinforced, only to be suddenly changed. This is in fact the weakness of William James's famous account of habit. He tells a possibly apocryphal story of an old soldier who overheard a command of 'Attention!' while carrying his dinner. He obeyed the command and dropped his food. James has also an account of how with the onset of adult life the character 'sets like plaster' due to the strength of habit. But of course just as many anecdotes (including true ones) can be told of dramatic or gradual developments in character into old age. As for reinforcement, one might easily have a habit, say, of eating in the same restaurant every day (primary reinforcement); then, possibly because of finding a better or cheaper one, or discovering that the old favourite

66

practices racial discrimination, change and never enter it again.

But we have wandered from the subject of pleasure. Hedonism had something of a revival when drive theories like Hull's began to appear inadequate, and seemed to be justified experimentally with the discovery of 'pleasure centres' in the brain. One of the difficulties with a purely homeostatic account of why people do things is that they obviously often do things that hardly seem to restore any sort of balance. They seek excess (see Chapter 4). So theorists have postulated some further seeking. Maslow wrote of self-actualization; McClelland of 'effective arousal'; and Young of 'positive affectivity'. R. S. Peters points out that such concepts do not help much as explanations. This is because they merely classify some behaviour as that which is not done for some reason beyond itself. To say that men create pictures or music is merely to state a fact: saying that they do so because of a need for self-actualization adds nothing. So with pleasure. Eating that satisfies hunger is usually pleasant; eating that does not can also be pleasant. Saying that the latter is done for pleasure merely means that it is not done for hunger (or other reasons) but because it, in itself, is pleasant. 'Pleasure' is not an explanation of why it is pleasant: some things are, and some are not.

Olds (1954) found that rats would press a bar indefinitely if the result was electrical stimulation of certain parts of the brain through implanted electrodes (see A2). These spots came to be known as pleasure centres. Of course this was quite misleading, since we have no way of knowing what the rats felt. You can do it with humans too, and there certainly are spots where it feels pleasant. But it does not follow that 'pleasure' was the cause of the bar pressing, partly for the reasons above and partly because one still can only *infer* what the rats felt. If human beings like to turn themselves on in this literal way, it seems no different in principle from eating sweets. It is a different matter if the electric current

67

were to cause the behaviour, cutting in directly on the normal circuits.

None of the concepts discussed should be taken as *the* explanation of behaviour, though this has been suggested in several cases. It is not just that it can be shown easily enough that reinforcement, for example, will not work in every case. It is that different *sorts* of behaviour call for different sorts of explanation.

Is there any general pattern?

Perhaps the commonest psychological answer to the question of why people act as they do has been the postulation of one or more instincts, drives, propensities, needs, motives, or what not. These may or may not be seen as the whole answer; they may be restricted to physiological, individual or social levels of behaviour; they may emphasize the past, present or future. And they may be ordered in various ways. Thus Freud's various versions of his instinct theory were cast as pairs of opposites: the sex drive and that for individual self-preservation; the life and death instincts McDougall's propensities ranged perhaps in order of human importance (from food-seeking to sneezing); Murray's needs and Maslow's, in order of satisfaction.

It is apparent that if a list is meant to cover all human activities, not only will it be endless, but it will lump together quite different sorts of activities. Is there any common factor? Certainly there can be no one mechanism that can count as an explanation for all. Rather, perhaps, we should look for one general sort of answer with a number of exceptions. That is the suggestion of R. S. Peters. The most obvious answer to the question why an individual acts is that he wants something, has some goal in mind, and some notion of how to reach it. This purposive rule-following model is, Peters argues, basic to explaining human behaviour

68

What the goals are, and what the rules are, will vary from individual to individual, and from culture to culture. It is the task of psychologists, anthropologists, and sociologists, according to Peters, to investigate these, sort them out, and present some orderly analysis. On the other hand much of what has recently passed for standard psychological explanation has in fact been concerned with exceptions. It is perfectly true that there are cases where behaviour is caused by physiological factors, such as hunger or brain damage; and there are other cases where a person is somehow compelled to do something, as with mental disorder. These are certainly the concern of Psychology, but they are to be regarded as deviations from the standard, obvious sort of explanation.

This comes out in Peters' discussion of Freud. Freud himself may, perhaps, never have been quite clear about some of the implications of his work. Freud was first of all a determinist; that is to say, he believed that human behaviour should and could receive a causal explanation. Dreams, to take an obvious example, were for Freud not mere oddities but mental events caused by other mental or psychological events, which ultimately could be shown to have a physiological basis. Equally they were not the result of occult or supernatural forces. And this applied to the whole of human behaviour.

Freud however started by attempting to cure neurotic symptoms, and then went on to try to explain his own success. His explanation was such that the neurotic was assimilated to the normal. The theory of psychoanalysis is that every child goes through essentially the same experiences, generating anxiety which is repressed and forming a pattern of development which determines later behaviour. In unfortunate cases, this results in illness. However, it seems there is no difference in principle between, say, an interest and an obsession. One man may prefer to live in the country, or become an explorer, another may suffer from claustrophobia (pathological fear of enclosed space). The explanation in each case is the same, the events of early childhood. There is simply a difference of degree.

The trouble with this is that the cases obviously are *not* the same in principle. Take the example of rationalization. This is a false reason given for an action, not with intent to deceive but because the person concerned does not know the real reason. For example, a suggestion may be given under hypnosis that later a subject will do some bizarre act, say recite a poem. Not infrequently, if asked why he did so, such a subject will offer a reason, such as that he felt bored, or thought it was relevant, or just wanted to. This is a rationalization, since the real reason is the post-hypnotic suggestion. The implication of psychoanalysis sometimes seems to be that all reasons are rationalizations. This makes little sense, since the concept of a 'rationalization' only has meaning by contrast with a real reason. To say that all offered reasons are rationalizations, and by extension that all behaviour is determined by unconscious factors, is like saying that all black is really white. One might well, actually, show that a given object that appeared black was really white, perhaps due to being in shadow etc. But the conclusion that all 'black' objects were really white would be false for two reasons: first, because however many individual cases are piled up, the next may not conform; but more basically because it would still be necessary to distinguish two categories of object, namely 'black' white and 'white' white.

So with behaviour. Even if much more of it than we thought is controlled by unconscious factors; and even if we can show how these operate in normal development: we must still distinguish that which is controlled from that which is not. The criterion must be something like this: whether the behaviour can be changed if a relevant reason is brought to bear. The explorer *can* decide to give up exploring, to stay at home and care for an invalid parent. The claustrophobe *cannot* stay in a small space, however sensible it is to do so.

Indeed this is precisely the point of psychoanalytic therapy: to increase the range of behaviour over which the individual has control. As Freud put it, 'where id was, there shall ego be'.

This does not mean that behaviour is not caused. It means that we must accept two sorts of cause: conscious and unconscious. Again this does not mean that behaviour is not caused, it means that it is sometimes not possible for us to be conscious of the cause.

Confusion over this seems to have led to a popular impression that psychological findings deny responsibility. It is far from uncommon to find magistrates, teachers, or parents angrily rejecting 'Psychology' on the grounds that it excuses the criminal or delinquent. Psychology does try to offer reasons for behaviour, but a reason is not in itself an excuse. It is true that some psychologists may have been confused about this. It is also true that it may be very difficult, in a particular case, to decide whether an individual could or could not have helped doing what he did. But to suppose that scientific explanation destroys responsibility is false. It *ought*, of course, to increase the area of responsibility, as some knowledge of the causes of behaviour becomes known.

It is said that during the First World War numbers of men were invalided out with what were known as gross hysterical symptoms: paralysis, or blindness, that prevented them fighting but which had no organic basis. In such cases there is no question of faking; the individual has no control over the symptoms. It is further said that such cases were much fewer in the 1939–45 war; and one may speculate on this being due to some wider general knowledge of unconscious motivation. The hypothesis is, of course, untestable.

It is plausible to suggest that at any one time, the sort of explanation of human behaviour that is generally acceptable is only partially related to the facts, in so far as they are known.

Thus in the mid-nineteenth century the psychologists, just beginning to distinguish themselves from philosophers, tended to think of reason as the normal mark of human conduct. It was not that no attention at all was paid to irrational or unconscious motivation. There were many writers on the unconscious before Freud. What Freud did, like Copernicus, was to change the centre of the system. He proposed that mental life – behaviour, if you like – was primarily unconscious. The further quality of consciousness might be present in favourable circumstances. Freud's views were at first resisted, then widely if loosely taken over. At the present time, cognitive factors in motivation have once more become popular (see D2 and D3).

A much more deep-rooted difference even than this is that between purposive and mechanical explanations. In classical Greece, the most far-reaching and profound analysis of human behaviour was offered by Aristotle (see F1 and F7). Aristotle's works, preserved by a series of flukes from the collapse of Greek scholarship, came for some centuries to dominate Western thought.

Aristotle of course was primarily a biologist, and couched many of his explanations of natural phenomena in biological terms: in terms of the nature, and the natural tendencies, of the thing in question. His doctrine of the four causes was meant to show what had to be taken into account in a full explanation. The material cause is that out of which something is made. The formal cause is a kind of ideal of the thing (rather like Plato's forms). The efficient cause is so to speak the mechanics, what propulsive forces lead to an event. The final cause is the goal or end towards which something is tending. It is the last two that are of particular importance for Psychology.

Applying this analysis to natural phenomena, Aristotle concluded that motion, for example, was to be explained by the goals towards which objects move, in virtue of their nature. Smoke rises, and heavy objects fall, because it is their nature to seek higher or lower goals respectively. This view, in the later Middle Ages, was progressively weakened, until with a last push Galileo overthrew it entirely, substituting the principle of inertia. By this, a body remains in motion until it is stopped by some opposing force. It is not aiming at anything. In Aristotle's terms, final causes were abandoned, and efficient causes became all that were acceptable.

Now this works rather well for the physical world, and on the basis of it massive advances were made, leading to an almost incredible degree of control over nature. When Psychology emerged as a separate discipline, it was not very surprising that it should try to model itself on the prestigious physical sciences which seemed, indeed, to be the pattern for all science. Thus the British Associationists produced their 'mental chemistry', the aim of which was to analyse the contents of the mind into basic units – ideas – and show how these linked up to form compound trains of thought. Wundt's German psychology had much the same programme for sensations. Freud produced a mental dynamics, followed by the hydraulic model of the ethologists. The Gestalt school preferred physics as the model, and Lewin a combination of that and topology.

Final causes have, on the whole, been regarded as non-respectable, though they figure in McDougall's theory. On Peters' analysis, it is more than time that they were rehabilitated. (It is also debatable whether Jungian archetypes can be seen as formal causes, and should likewise have another innings. Or, perhaps, the self Maslow wishes to actualize. See Chapter 6.) This emphasis is quite deep in its effects. If one is told, for example, that a man rigged an election in order to achieve office (say), is there not a tendency to reply 'But what was the *real* reason?'

But it is not just one type of scientific explanation that is favoured. The prevailing ethos is that scientific explanation as such is preferable. It does not seem sufficient reason for this that it just is preferable. For how much more successful have our 'scientific' explanations been than those of the past? To talk of the mentally ill as possessed by devils seems absurd: yet they occupy half the hospital beds in the country.

It is difficult to see how explanations of human behaviour can ever be divorced from values. This is not just a matter of some models being fashionable, nor even for the reasons given in Chapter 1. It is also that people do things because of values. This is more apparent when we consider the personhood qualities of individuals. We have mentioned the self-concept. McDougall wrote of the 'self-regarding sentiment': the organization of feeling and intellect against which we match our own performance. The concept attracts little attention now. Values are studied to some extent, but as little more than interests: possibly because in a relativistic age the notion of doing things because they seem right is somewhat unfashionable.

RK: Perhaps I could add my opionion that the 'psychology of motivation' seems to me a good example of what Wittgenstein (1953) was referring to when he wrote:

> The confusion and barrenness of psychology is not to be explained by calling it a 'young science'; its state is not comparable with that of physics, for instance, in its beginnings . . . For in psychology there are experimental methods and *conceptual confusion* . . . The existence of the experimental method makes us think we have the means of solving the problem which

74

troubles us; though method and problem pass one another by.

JR: What do you think is the conceptual confusion here?
RK: There are many examples. One is the 'reification' of the major terms: 'reinforcement', 'motivation', 'reward', etc. begin as operational definitions of observed behaviour and end up in some twilight zone between being a theory, an explanation and a problem. Another problem is the premature application of experimental methods. Experiment without adequate conceptual clearing is like a headless horseman. Thirdly the 'theories of motivation' are apparently dealing with different phenomena, concerning different species, express themselves in mutually exclusive data languages, and in any case never seem to state exactly what they are supposed to be theories *of*. Hence it is difficult to assess their value.

4
Emotions: do they help or hinder?

The closer we get to human aspects of Psychology, the more elusive they become. We find ourselves in a Looking-Glass world where the straight path suddenly twists and turns, and we end up walking away from the objective.

On first consideration nothing seems simpler than feelings and emotions. Anger or despair may be hard to tolerate, but there is no problem about understanding them. Milder emotions such as sympathy and happiness are familiar to every normal human being. It is when we try to give some conceptual analysis, or carry out experimental investigations, that we enter a maze of problems. As yet, no-one has found a satisfactory path through the maze, and every theorist has ended up breaking the walls of the maze to get out: that is to say, ignoring or twisting the facts.

One of the most obvious points about emotions, apart from the apparent fact that we all share them, would seem to be that they cause behaviour. Why did X shoot his wife, or himself? Because he was jealous, or unhappy. Why did Y slam the door? Because he was angry.

This apparently obvious view was turned on its head in what came to be perhaps the most famous theory of emotion, that of William James (1842–1910) (see A2). It was known as the James-Lange theory since Carl Lange, a Danish physiologist, published almost the same theory a year after James (1884; 1885). Briefly the theory was that certain situations cause us to react in certain ways. These reactions are accompanied by specific bodily changes, and it is the awareness of these changes that constitutes an emotion. In James's famous example, a man sees a bear, and runs away or prepares to. This involves muscles tightening, stomach contracting, etc.; and the experience of these effects is what we call fear.

This theory became extremely influential, and much work was devoted to attacking or defending it. Most of James's defence was based on introspection: he argued, for example, that if you imagine some strong emotion, such as anger, and then try to strip it of all its bodily components, there will be nothing left to imagine.

One objection to this might be that it does not work so well for some less strong feelings, say, the mild sympathy one might experience if giving to a street beggar. This argument unlocks a Pandora's box of problems about what counts as emotion. Hastily closing it, another objection could be the unreliable – some would say unacceptable – nature of introspective evidence, though the present authors do not accept this.

The main objections came from Walter Cannon. He based his attack on experimental evidence, and stressed the following points, among others. Changes in the viscera (the internal organs of stomach, intestines, etc.) can be induced artificially, and do not then seem to be accompanied by emotion. On the other hand if the connections between the viscera and the nervous system are severed, emotions can still occur. The viscera are in any case relatively insensitive, and sensations from them could not be the basis of the whole subtle range of emotion. Moreover they react slowly, whereas feelings often seem to occur almost instantly on perception of a particular situation.

Such arguments seemed for a time to put paid to the James-Lange theory. More recently it has made a comeback. First of all it is pointed out that James did not deal just with the visceral organs, but with the whole complex of bodily reactions. Some of these are both rapid and exact. One of the best examples is the face. The human face is closely involved in emotions. Facial expression is one of the chief cues for interpreting another's feelings, but expression is not easy to control voluntarily. Anyone who has tried to act convincingly, or had the problem of 'keeping a straight face' will agree. There is some evidence (e.g. Izard, 1971) that artificial induction of a smile or frown is accompanied by the appropriate feeling. On the other hand patients suffering from pathological laughter due to certain sorts of brain damage are often by no means amused – but then, one might say, who would be? Their sensations must be an extraordinary complex of competing emotions. So the maze winds on.

The main support for James comes from studies showing that the viscera are, in fact, more important in emotion than Cannon thought. We shall refer to some of the evidence in a moment.

The James-Lange theory, apart from containing a good deal of truth, does bring out several of the puzzles about emotion. There is first the relationship with motivation, and indeed the role of emotions in the whole sequence of behaviour. There is the problem of what is to count as an emotion. There is the fact that, whatever does, at least three components have to be reckoned with: the physiological, the experiential, and the cognitive. And there is the question whether there is something peculiarly human about emotions.

Components of emotion

In some ways the physiological basis of emotion seems an attractive starting point (see A2), partly because it is more obvious than with some aspects of behaviour, and partly because of the ever-present lure of reductionism (see p. 19). In fact the position is far from clear. Cannon's theory stressed the neurophysiology of emotion and particularly the role of the thalamus (a subcortical structure). The thalamus was thought to receive information from the cortex when some situation was perceived, and respond with particular processes according to the emotion involved. These aroused the muscles and viscera. Subsequent evidence shows that this is too simple, and many theorists have tried to tie together the known and speculative facts.

Gellhorn, for example, argues that we have to deal with two basic and opposing types of activity; work-directed and rest-directed. These are maintained in balance, the basis of emotion being an integration of bodily responses and activity of the autonomic nervous system. It is impossible to evaluate the complex experimental evidence here. Indeed when this is done, as by Strongman (1973), the only possible conclusion is that several different physiological components are all involved in emotion, but that we do not as yet really know how.

While this may be depressing for the physiologist, it does not necessarily affect the psychological issues. For example the discovery of the so-called pleasure centres in the brain at first promised a rapid breakthrough to understanding of both motivation and emotion. In fact, it is merely one more piece of evidence that a particular part of the nervous system may be involved (not *must* be, for this process might not be the normal one).

Several of the older theorists tried to integrate emotion with other aspects of behaviour by using the concept of *instinct*. This is one of those concepts, so frequent in Psychology, that for a time seem to explain everything, then are debunked and thought useless, and then, it may be, revived in modified form. It has attracted those who, in opposition to a mechanical behaviourism, have felt that one of the chief puzzles about behaviour is to explain why it is apparently purposeful. The behaviour of mobile organisms, as one moves up the evolutionary scale, seems increasingly to be aimed at something. Jellyfish just drift; dogs hunt; men plan and build. Even the play of very small children does not look aimless or random. Indeed purpose has often been said to be a defining characteristic of behaviour; and it would seem odd to think of a randomly acting organism as in any sense a person.

William McDougall (1871–1938) made instincts or propensities his key concept. Behaviour was to be explained as sets of tendencies to continue in a certain direction until some goal was reached. Each propensity was accompanied by its characteristic emotion. As with Maslow's hierarchy of needs, the propensities range from basic to higher; but also from universal (like eating) to, as it were, optional (like self-abasement). The system has many weaknesses, but does at least try to integrate motives, feelings, and cognition, as must eventually be done.

The same is true of Freud, a more famous instinct theorist. As often with Freud, his views progressively changed as he went on, making it sometimes hard to know what were his final conclusions. Emotions are closely linked with instinctive energy, the source of which is unconscious. But it is not clear whether they are themselves to be considered as forms of energy or as signs or accompaniments of it. Another puzzle concerns unconscious emotions. One can see that a conscious feeling must have unconscious sources, for we certainly do not always know why we feel strongly about something. But psychoanalytic theory seems to imply that there are also feelings we are not aware of.

This is odd in so far as awareness is usually part of what we mean by 'feeling'. And it is not clear whether the usual physiological processes are supposed to operate. Thus the theory deals with unconscious anxiety: but anxiety normally considered involves a beating heart, sweating palms, etc. Possibly it is better to think of a sort of mechanism of anxiety, ready to be reactivated whenever the present situation sufficiently resembles the original one.

However this may be, psychoanalysis, and many other therapeutic techniques, involve becoming more aware of one's own feelings. Here as elsewhere in psychology chasms stretch between common sense, traditional practice, experimental testing, and theoretical problems. Common sense or observation tells us that we can think about our feelings, that we can become more sensitive or alert to them, and that some people are better at this than others. Many people who experience joy or serenity from music must recall a time before they did so, and the process of learning finer discriminations. What we might call traditional practices – therapy, but also the older techniques of meditation and prayer – are certainly out of common experience, yet their history suggests they are in some way natural. 'Primitive' societies use dreams and magic to (among other things) reveal the feelings and desires of an individual. Experimental investigation, on the other hand, is remarkably difficult. How can the effects be measured? What sort of operational definition can be given of 'self-awareness'? Here a recent new approach has been the development of *biofeedback*. Modern technology makes it possible, for the first time, actually to have direct knowledge of many of the physiological components of emotion, such as the electrical activity of the brain. And, it seems, to bring about changes in them.

Proponents of biofeedback, which has become something of a cult, wish to link its effects with those of the older methods such as the exercises and meditation of yoga.

This is yet unproved, as is the real nature of the results claimed.

Partly due to some of the theoretical problems, the value of introspective reports is (we think) established, but only if they can be linked with other evidence. In the case of feelings, there is the further apparently insoluble problem of knowing whether two people's feelings are the same. Again a fairly common occurrence must be the having of a profound experience, and the conviction that the feelings of others, despite what they do or say, are not the same (or indeed *are* the same – the evidence is no better). Theoretically it seems impossible even to know that another person has any feelings at all: yet such a conclusion appears absurd.

In practice, of course, each individual constantly interprets what he sees of others in terms of their feelings. Just how this is done is only beginning to be explored experimentally. The most obvious source of information is verbal. Emotions are expressed both directly and indirectly in speech. Equally obviously, this is not enough. There must at least be some consistency of behaviour, and some other sources of knowledge such as the history or circumstances of the individual. ('She says she's perfectly happy, but I don't think she is.')

In recent years much attention has been given to non-verbal communication. Darwin (1872) argued that the mechanisms of this – such as frowning, smiling, etc. – originated in just the same evolutionary way as other characteristics, namely by serving a function; and then remained as vestiges when the function diminished. Clenching the fist in anger, for example, survives as a rudimentary attack. This approach has lately been taken up again by, for example, Eibl-Eibesfeldt (1970). However, the general idea now is that behaviour which serves to communicate between individuals becomes 'ritualized' (a technical term, the central meaning of which is perhaps 'set' or 'stereotyped'). It is risky to stretch this approach to human behaviour, but there are several points of interest.

One is that in strong emotion people do perhaps fall into set ways of expression. (This does not seem to have been investigated systematically.) Another is the need to study the detailed process of the communication of emotion. Argyle (1969) and others, for example, have tried to analyse the effects of nonverbal cues in face-to-face interaction: eye contact, facial expression, movement, and gesture. It does not appear as yet that any new general theory has emerged.

In fact, we can agree with Strongman that the only firm conclusion to be drawn is that in some way expression of emotion is apprehended almost immediately and intuitively. 'Intuition' is not a popular word with psychologists, who tend to see it as merely covering up their own ignorance. However, unless we believe in thought transference, it must be that emotion is conveyed from one person to another by means of cues that can, in principle, be analysed. How subtle these must be can be seen if one tries to say just why the performance of one actor is great, while another in the same part is mediocre; or compares a good traditional singer with a concert artist. Subjectively (JR) what happens in the latter case is that the traditional singer seems to live the events of the song, and by some ineffable art causes one to, as it were, fall into step and share that re-created experience.

One of the few attempts to experiment on this kind of empathic grasp of another's feelings has been made by Stotland (1969). He measured his subject's reactions by their palm sweating and blood flow and by having them rate their own feelings. They watched an accomplice of the experimenter who was supposedly experiencing a painful or pleasant or neutral stimulus. The subjects were asked either to imagine how they would feel in the accomplice's place; or to imagine how he felt; or to watch his physical reactions closely. Stotland found that the first two produced changes in his subjects' responses, but not the third.

This perhaps does not take us very far in investigating empathy, except to show again that it can exist. It does lead us to a third important component of emotion, its *contextual determinants*. These have been rather dramatically brought to the fore in some experiments by Stanley Schachter which are in a way the converse of Stotland's. Schachter (1970) started from the assumption that emotions cannot be differentiated on the basis of their physiological component alone: an individual must have additional information in order to recognize an emotion. To test this, Schachter used in several experiments injections of epinephrine, a substance that produces physical effects like those of general arousal: rise in blood pressure, increased heart rate, respiration and level of blood sugar. Subjects were under the impression that they were testing a drug for its effects on eyesight. Different groups were told to expect side-effects – either the true effects or opposite ones – or no side-effects.

The ingenious part was that while subjects were supposedly waiting for the eyesight tests to begin, they were joined by a stooge, who either played about in a boisterous, rather silly way, or displayed anger over a questionnaire both were completing. Subjects were watched while all this was going on, and later filled in a questionnaire including concealed items about mood. On the whole, the general arousal due to the epinephrine appeared in the subjects' behaviour and responses as euphoria (elation) or anger. Schachter has reported several other experiments with the general conclusion that how we label emotions is largely a *cognitive* matter: the physiology is much the same in each case.

These experiments became famous, but are open to several objections. Methodological criticisms were made by Plutchik and Ax (1967) – and this is a good example of just how careful experiments need to be. First, it was not clear whether the experimenters knew which groups of subjects were which. If they did this could influence the results (the 'experimenter effect'). Second, it is well established that epinephrine affects individuals in widely different ways: there was no guarantee that the groups were equally matched for this. Third, the questions subjects were asked afterwards were ambiguous. Fourth, other experiments found that subjects in the 'euphoric' situation could interpret feelings in several different ways, including opposite ones such as disgust or anger. And so on.

All these points could be overcome by careful planning. Another sort of criticism might be that hardly anyone would doubt that emotions must involve a contextual element. Indeed in *some* cases it seems odd to speak of the emotion at all without this. (Imagine someone angry. 'What are you angry about?' 'Nothing, I'm just angry.') On the other hand emotions can certainly change without any change in the situation. Depression can be lifted by drugs or even a good meal. There is nothing more to feel cheerful about than there was before; but things just don't look so bad.

In general, though, human beings experience emotions in response to situations, which are assessed in a complex way. This is one reason why it seems not to make sense to say that animals feel as we do. They cannot regret the past or hope for the future, just two of the simplest factors in human emotions. Some theorists, notably Magda Arnold and Richard Lazarus, make 'appraisal' the central concept in understanding emotion, though perhaps without any very clear notion of where to go from there.

What counts as an emotion

One cause of disagreement over which most writers have stubbed their toes is the definition of emotions. They do this by trying to include explanations in their definitions, or by limitations that turn out to be inconsistent, or by drawing up lists that seem either too long or too short. The fallacy is to think that a phenomenon must be defined before it can be investigated. Strongman is one who wisely presents the evidence first before offering his own approach to definition, which is, roughly, the 'feeling' components of the reaction to any stimulus, it being supposed that there always are some, even if almost unnoticeable.

However this may be, it is another matter to try to map out the emotions, rather as Eysenck or Cattell try to do for personality traits (see D3), or Guilford for intelligence (see D4). Plutchik (1962) for example gives us a multidimensional model of the emotions. Plutchik considers there are eight basic dimensions, which each vary from very low to very high intensity. At the low end of each dimension is sleep, but as the dimensions become more intense they also get more distinct, the eight intense ends being: vigilance, loathing, grief, terror, amazement, acceptance, ecstasy, rage. (They sound like characters in a medieval mystery play.) Drawn, the model looks like half an orange, cut through its equator. This model is supported by studies in which names of emotions were rated for their degree of intensity and distance from each other. This model raises several questions. At first sight it looks rather like a colour spectrum; but of course the difference is that the spectrum represents wavelengths of light, which can be objectively determined. No-one has yet demonstrated how this could be done for human feelings (or any other psychological characteristics). Then again it is not clear if this is how people conceive of emotions in general, or their own emotions, or neither. Subjectively it would seem that one's own emotional 'model' would be rather like early maps of the known world: familiar parts in some detail, distant parts distorted or missing. We can undoubtedly explore more of our emotional world, but it is not clear whether we could reach the end of it.

RK: Of course not. The model must be one of the expanding universe.

How emotions develop

We do not really know how emotions develop. One of the most influential accounts, still found in many textbooks, was that of Bridges (1932). She considered that at birth a child is capable of showing only a general excitement or arousal. By the age of three months it is possible to distinguish positive and negative feelings – distress and delight. As development proceeds, these in turn separate out into, or from them branch out, more and more finely discriminated emotions. While this seems quite plausible, it was based on observations rather than experiment. The definitions used were inadequate, and so were the observations of the newly born child.

Nevertheless subsequent accounts tend to support the idea of progressive differentiation, and this accords with common sense. The problem is that we do not know how this comes about. It is not easy to carry out controlled experiments on the emotional development of children. Even if there were not strong ethical reasons against it, it would be an extremely complex matter to control the variables. Animal studies, on the other hand, have often been well controlled: but the difficulty is that emotion is largely a human phenomenon.

Partly to overcome this, H. F. Harlow carried out what has become a very famous series of experiments using rhesus monkeys, which are at least closer to us than laboratory rats. Harlow's main technique was to rear infant monkeys with various sorts of substitute for the real mother. These surrogates were models made of wire, roughly the size of adult monkeys. A model might be of bare wire, or covered with cloth; it might include a nipple giving milk; it might provide

87

movement by means of a rocking base. In this way Harlow hoped to isolate just which features of the mother were sought by the infant, and which were necessary for normal development. He found, for example, that an infant monkey would cling to a cloth mother without milk in preference to a wire mother with it. Perhaps not very surprising, except to rigid behaviourists who might want to relate everything to 'primary reinforcers' such as food.

Harlow's general conclusions were that an emotional relationship develops between infant and mother, based on a combination of feeding, comfort, and support; and that this, and its subsequent extension to play with other infants, is necessary for normal adult growth. Monkeys reared without mothers, for example, fail to develop normal social and sexual behaviour with other adults. Infants reared together with no mother spent long periods clinging to each other.

Furthermore it appeared that experiences must take place at certain periods – the three-to-six-month age being 'critical'. These results agreed well with the general notion of 'imprinting' familiar from studies of animals in natural conditions. In the well-known examples of Konrad Lorenz, greylag goslings developed a following response to the first object seen after hatching, namely himself. This was said to influence later mating behaviour. Subsequent controlled experiment has shown, as so often, that none of the effects are quite as neat as was first thought. In any case, imprinting is not an explanation, but something to be explained.

Harlow's work also fits nicely with Freud's remark that a mother's task was to teach her son to love; and with the psychoanalytically inspired work of John Bowlby. While it is not yet possible to say certainly just what are all the necessary conditions for normal emotional development in humans, it is a reasonable assumption that there needs to be a reasonably stable, warm relationship with one or more adults. This should allow the child to explore the limits of affection; to add new experiences while having, as it were, a safe base to fall back on. (Some of Harlow's films show infant monkeys doing just this.) Some would see here a superiority of a relaxed and varied 'extended family' over the sometimes limited and rigid family pattern of our society.

Psychoanalytic theory does at least attempt to suggest the mechanisms of emotional development. One important aspect is internalization. It is supposed that a child, at first unconsciously, models himself upon the important adults around him; or rather upon his necessarily distorted perception of them. Aronfreed (1968) among others has developed this. He supposes that, given an initial attachment to an adult, the child will so to speak monitor his own behaviour as if he were the adult. For example if affection is withdrawn or seems to be withdrawn the child becomes self-critical, blaming himself for the loss.

There are few attempts to investigate this sort of mechanism experimentally. For example Grusec (1966) had five and six year olds in three groups. An experimenter either was affectionate, or cold, or first affectionate and then cold. A game was arranged that went wrong in such a way that each child thought it was his fault. It appeared that the 'warm' group were more self-critical than the 'cold'; but only the 'warm-then-cold' group carried their self-criticism over into new situations. It is instructive to compare this with the treatent of political prisoners. (See Chapter 5.)

The function of emotions

At first sight it seems that one of the most obvious characteristics of emotion is that it disrupts behaviour. Grief and rage render people less capable of considered action than they are usually. The common saying 'count to ten' to an angry person exemplifies this.

Several theorists feel that this is a misleading view. R. W. Leeper (1948) argues that it is left over from the rationalist conception of the nature of man that came to the fore in the eighteenth century and persisted through the nineteenth. With Freud, the emotions were once more the object of study, but their influence was a disruptive one.

Leeper argues in contrast that emotions do not disrupt behaviour but rather organize and motivate it. There is some degree of emotion in all behaviour, and it is this that gives it direction, enabling us to choose between alternatives or solve problems. He points out that the concept of 'disorganization' is a confused one. For example, a man in extreme fear may not be able to continue with what he was doing: but his body, at least, is quickly alerted, and well organized, for 'fight or flight' – increased activity of muscles and heart, less of stomach, etc. Similarly he may think more quickly of plans and resources. It is only in very extreme cases that appropriate behaviour is inhibited. Emotions, on Leeper's view, are part of a continuum from physiological needs or motives through to the purely emotional type of motive. This is only one view, and it has not, as yet, attracted much experimental evidence.

Another 'organizing' view is that of P. T. Young, who stresses that emotions provoke action, they lead the organism to do something. They tend to sustain behaviour until a goal is reached, and then terminate it (rather like McDougall's propensities). But they also organize behaviour by influencing the formation of 'neurobehavioural patterns' that become learned.

Arguments and evidence can be found to show that emotions both help and hinder. No theory as yet has managed to fit in all the available facts to make one coherent picture. As far as general anxiety goes, there is some approach to regularity in the Yerkes-Dodson Law. This principle, dating back to 1908, is that too little or too much drive (anxiety) lead to poorer performance on tasks of various kinds. The optimal level is in the middle, giving a U-shaped curve. However the optimal level varies with type of task: the more complex it is, the lower the level of drive for best performance. Even this arrangement, while true over a range of experiments, has not been shown in single subjects. And when the whole range of emotions is considered, no such regularity appears.

One thing that seems rather obviously true is that, for whatever reason, human beings have a lot of emotion. As far as we have any means of telling, the range and depth of human emotions far exceeds that found in other living things. Probably, if such a calculation made sense, the total 'amount' of emotion would exceed the amount of cognition, in the sense that most lives are dominated far more by feeling than by reflection or logic. Individuals certainly vary in breadth and depth of emotion, though this has not been very exactly investigated. Animals can be selectively bred for emotionality, and doubtless in humans genetic differences interact in a complex way with environmental factors. Families and cultures vary widely in their attitude to emotional life, often giving rise to popular stereotypes such as the 'stiff upper lip' English or the dramatic Latins. However, openness of expression may or may not be related to inner feeling.

Individuals do seem to differ in their ability to judge the feelings of others. Little has suggested that some people are 'thing specialists', others 'person specialists'. The latter use more words, but fewer dimensions, to describe people. On the whole women tend to describe other people in terms of personality, men in terms of roles, achievement, and physical characteristics. Adolescent girls, however, stress physical traits such as hair colour and height. Emotions, of course, are only part of such person perception (see B2) – a part of both the perceiver and the perceived – but it has been assumed that increased sensitivity of feeling can contribute to better judgments and understanding of others.

Various techniques have been offered to train in social skills. Argyle (1969) lists nine main approaches. The most effective, he concludes, is probably role-playing. In this, an individual practices the 'part' he wishes to become better at, and gets feedback from a skilled instructor, and/or an audience, and/or video-tape playback. The role might be part of a job, such as interviewing, or it might be a life-role such as mother. A variation is role-reversal, where a husband and wife, or lecturer and student, change parts temporarily.

Such an approach, concentrating systematically on specific skills, seems much preferable to some of the more widely publicized methods of sensitivity training, for example T-groups (T = training). Here groups of about twelve individuals meet for a series of two-hour sessions, say fifteen or twenty in two weeks. The main activity is to study the processes of interaction in the group itself, and this is backed up by lectures, discussions, etc. The aims are to improve perception of self and others, attitudes to others, work effectiveness, and several other traits. Research on the results of such groups shows that while some 30-40 per cent of participants may benefit, others are seriously disturbed. And there is no conclusive evidence that what benefits there are result from the T-group experience itself, or that they could not be got by other means.

Thus one is bound to feel highly sceptical about rather unsupported claims for even more drastic and uncontrolled techniques such as have been proliferating for some time under various titles such as encounter groups, sensitivity training, creativity workshops, etc. (see B1 and F3). There are some differences between these (see for example *Encounter Groups* by Carl Rogers, 1969), but all have in common some sort of intensive group experience, in which individuals reveal their feelings to each other and seek to become aware of the psychological processes operating in themselves and in the group. It is as yet impossible to reach firm conclusions about these based on research, for a whole variety of reasons. Controlled research is felt by some to miss the point; the aims are often vaguely stated; subjects and procedures are highly variable.

Perhaps the most striking thing about such groups is rapid rise to popularity, suggesting (as Rogers remarks) that they supply something not found in family, work, or social organizations. Such shared experiences do find a place in most cultures, often in an aesthetic or spiritual context. Our own offers little more than the crude device of the football match.

In a somewhat similar way, perhaps, individuals seek means to attain extremes of emotion. Such feats as sailing alone around the world or climbing Everest do produce extremes of despair and ecstasy, as is apparent from personal accounts. Perhaps it is not too fanciful to group here at least some aspects of dangerous drug-taking and reckless driving. What we know of those who have achieved great things suggests often that at some period of development they have pushed themselves, in one emotional direction or another, as far as they can go. If true, the relationship between experience and achievement remains to be elucidated.

Certainly it is not clear whether emotional experience alone, even if dramatic, necessarily leads to personal development. A life too full of emotion can distort the perception of reality. Autonomy and identity presumably are related to the integration of rational and irrational. And we should not mistake the dramatic for the effective. It would be a mistake to assume that the emotional life of Tolstoy was *necessarily* richer or more intense than that of Emily Dickinson.

Range and depth of feeling would very likely be nominated by many people as what makes us particularly human. Science fiction, which in some ways provides a modern counterpart of mythology, gives us by way of contrast the robot and the alien. Just as the burden of myth, if the structuralists are right, is to distinguish man from the animals, so the typical non-human of the machine age is devoid of feeling, though it may equal or surpass man in intelligence.

Philosophers certainly think it worthwhile to argue whether a robot could have feelings or an alien be human, concluding, as often as not, that it all depends on what you mean.

RK: It certainly doesn't *all* depend on what you mean. It depends on whether you can assert that man has some characteristic or group of characteristics that distinguishes him from other things and beings. I believe we can say this, and that the distinguishing feature lies in his conjunction of consciousness and affect. By 'consciousness' I mean to include certain capacities which man alone, it seems, possesses. In particular, his ability to 'go beyond the information given', as Bruner puts it; to represent an absent environment; to transform and transcend his experience; in short to *imagine*.

JR: I don't think any psychologist would deny this, though I am not so sure about the uniqueness. Animals can certainly represent the absent environment to some extent – they can remember. And it is just evolutionary chance that man has no really close surviving relatives.

RK: That doesn't affect my argument – the fact is that man does have this capacity. Further he has a capacity for a certain sort of awareness, which I will call spiritual in a pure sense. This is the apotheosis or highest attainment of feeling. Its enjoyment, I suspect, is the highest goal of man. It is what the great mystics of all periods have sought: the contemplation and enjoyment of a reality that lies behind appearances. This reality is characterized by order, beauty, and love. It is the quintessence of all religions to savour the hidden order of beauty in reality; and evidence could be quoted from innumerable sources.

JR: Of course I don't wish to deny that many people throughout history have said this, or something like it. And for an equally long period, others have denied its importance. Very likely it comes down to a matter of preference. But there are several things about it that worry me.

One is that belief in mystical revelation doesn't seem to have any very consistent or productive effects on behaviour. Mystics may withdraw themselves into contemplation, in which case they may find ecstasy or Nirvana, but this doesn't seem to be very helpful to the rest of us. Or alternatively they may try to propagate their ideas. And then they come out with such varied programmes that one cannot believe they have all had access to the same hidden order of reality. And if some have got it wrong, how do we know that any have got it right?

RK: As usual you're missing the point ...

JR: Wait, let me finish. Furthermore the only evidence brought forward is the individual's own experience, which is not sufficient to convince me. What it seems to do is render the individual immune to reason or evidence, and, in some cases, determined to impose his ideas on others. I fear and dislike fanatics of all persuasions. I prefer the Florence of Lorenzo de Medici to that of Savonarola, and the England of Shakespeare to that of the Puritans. If that is what you mean by the apotheosis of affect, I think it a poor guide to conduct.

RK: You omit to mention 'practical mysticism'. The Bhagavad Gita, the principal sacred text in Hindu culture, actually enjoins the reader to perform selfless action in the world, *after* attaining Nirvana. Buddhists, too, tread the 'Noble Eightfold Path' in action, not selfish withdrawal. Selfish mysticism is in a minority compared with self*less*, practical mysticism.

Secondly, you don't state what the goals of conduct and action may be. It is surely widely held that the propagation and contemplation of beauty, art, love and wisdom are candidates. Practical mysticism is conducive to the attainment of these goals.

JR: So you assert.

5
Can the person be destroyed?

All too easily: but what is it that might be destroyed? As has been suggested, the polymorphous concept of the person has at least three attributes, the loss of any one of which tends to diminish personhood. They are the sense of personal identity; the ability to act autonomously, i.e. not 'controlled; and contact with reality. These are to an extent linked to each other, but not indissolubly so. It seems that they can be disturbed in reverse order of ease, as it were a castle whose outer walls may fall while the inner still resist. The sense of identity is like the keep, the last and strongest refuge.

Thus contact with reality can be disturbed quite easily, even by mild drugs. We all lose it in sleep, and in any case it is never absolute (see Chapter 1). But to the extent that it *is* lessened, by so much are we less a person. At the other end, even in severely disturbed or deprived states some awareness of oneself seems to develop, or persist. If that is extinguished, it no longer seems sense to speak of there being a person.

RK: There you go as usual, proceeding entirely by argument. Where are the facts?

JR: I thought it was *your* job to supply them. Anyway what I assert is the result of my wide reading – don't you think the reader is entitled to the benefit?

RK: !

JR: You'd better save your expostulations for Chapter 6, you'll really need them there.

Injury and illness

Almost any injury or illness tends to diminish personhood (which is not to say that individuals do not sometimes surpass themselves in response to adversity). Some disturbances are more specific in their effects than others. Physical handicaps necessarily reduce autonomy (see F2); severe pain tends to restrict the horizon of awareness, while pain-killing drugs lessen contact with reality.

Illnesses are commonly divided into organic and functional, according to whether we can or cannot point to a physiological basis. The distinction is not a fundamental one, for every illness must have both a physical substrate and psychological effects. However we can start by mentioning specific areas of the brain, injury to which has very clear effects.

Many of these have been explored by A. R. Luria, the great Russian psychologist. He has shown, for example, that the function of organizing visual stimuli, so that they are perceived as meaningful wholes, is carried out in what are known as the secondary zones of the visual cortex. A patient with injury here sees individual items but cannot make sense of them. Luria (1973) quotes a patient puzzling over a picture, identifying two circles and a cross-bar, and concluding it must be a bicycle; it was a pair of spectacles. Other examples were interpreting a cock with coloured tail feathers as a fire, or a telephone with a dial as a clock.

The sensory cortex is a relatively 'primitive' part of the

brain in terms of evolution. The most advanced parts are the frontal lobes. These, Luria shows, are crucial to human conscious activity. To give only one example, a patient with a tumour affecting both lobes was asked to draw two triangles and a minus sign. He did so, but the minus appeared as a rectangle. Asked next to draw a circle, he included another rectangle inside it – and inside the rectangle the words 'no entry'. It could be said that what he had lost was his ability to form and carry out an appropriate plan – which involves checking what is done against reality.

Conversely it is possible to elicit fairly specific behaviour patterns by direct stimulation of the normal brain. Electrodes can be permanently implanted in the brain, with terminals outside the scalp ready for use. This permits the stimulation, for example, of the now well-known 'pleasure' and 'pain' areas. To receive or avoid such stimulation animals will work incessantly; while in humans strong emotions are aroused – or at least simulated, for emotions are partly defined by their context (see Chapter 4). The result certainly seems to reduce the human status: as one subject put it, 'I don't know what came over me. I felt like an animal' (Heath, Monroe, and Mickle, 1955). In another case quoted by Delgado (1969), electrical stimulation of the right temporal lobe produced amatory advances towards the therapist (the subject was a patient suffering from severe epilepsy which had resisted all previous treatment).

Delgado argues that the increase of knowledge gained by these means will reduce suffering and increase human happiness. This may be so, but the possibilities of abuse are no longer a science fiction fantasy.

Similar arguments apply to the multitude of new (and some of the old) drugs that have behavioural effects. Alcohol has been a component of most civilizations known to us and I (JR) would be among the last to deny its virtues; but that it produces loss of self-control is a matter of folklore, common experience, and experimental data. Addiction, of course, results in severe personal deterioration and the same is true of more drastic substances such as heroin. So-called 'truth' drugs reduce the capacity for autonomous action. The effect of 'psychedelic' drugs, which appear to be non-addictive, is debatable. Users claim that personal development is enhanced, but the meaning of this is not very clear. There is no firm evidence that users are more creative in any testable sense. They *may* be more aware of their own feelings and motives: but claims usually seem to rest on the notion of perception of another, mystical reality (see Chapter 6).

The extreme abandonment of personhood might be said to be suicide. Actually, it is well established (e.g. Braaten, 1963) that the large majority of suicide attempts are not meant to succeed. They are cries for help in some intolerable situation. In general self-inflicted injury is intended to be temporary.

The same cannot be said of mental disorder (see F3). In particular, the disorders classed as 'schizophrenia', which probably constitute those most destructive of the personality. The varied symptoms are nowadays usually masked by drugs, so that the typical patient seems merely rather apathetic. In the natural state, as it were, some common features emerge, involving a deterioration of the whole personality. The patient becomes progressively less able to deal with reality, which may be distorted by hallucinations or delusions (false beliefs). The capacity for appropriate emotions seems to be lost, as is that for planning and carrying out action. Awareness of time and place are often lost. Above all, perhaps, there seems to be a loss of the sense of personal identity. It is this, probably, that gives rise to the popular notion of the man who thinks he is Napoleon. It is as though the patient, unable to know who he is, clutches feebly at an identification with some powerful and relatively stable figure.

The causes of schizophrenia are unknown. This is not for want of either hypotheses or research. Most investigators seem to have concentrated on some particular aspect which, while important, leaves us still in doubt as to an explanation. Thus psychoanalysis suggests a regression to a very early stage of infantile behaviour. Social psychologists stress the breakdown in communication. Cognitive theorists study the disorders of attention or concept formation. Existentially-inclined writers hold that the patient is making a reasonable response to unbearable pressures of home or society; while others think that it is all a matter of convention, of what particular behaviour a society agrees to call 'mad'. Among the few well established facts seem to be that there is some kind of hereditary element in at any rate the *disposition* to develop schizophrenic symptoms; and that the same sort of symptoms are found across a wide range of cultures.

Schizophrenia is sometimes referred to as 'split personality'. This is a mistake, arising from a misunderstanding of the theories of Bleuler (1911) who coined the word 'schizophrenia'.

Rare cases of 'split' or 'multiple' personality have been reported, one of the more famous being *The Three Faces of Eve* (Thigpen and Cleckley, 1957). In such cases one individual seems to live two lives, typically showing two sorts of behaviour. At least one of the 'personalities' is unaware of the actions of the other(s). Again there is no good explanatory theory. Perhaps such cases can best be regarded as extreme exaggeration of the normal separation of parts of life from each other. One does not let every event at home, for example, intrude into work. Society often imposes formal or informal taboos of this kind. The arrangement becomes pathological when the individual is actually *unable* to cross the frontiers.

Society and the individual

It is difficult to see how a person could develop, or perhaps exist for long, without some form of society (see Chapter 2).

But both society and the individual have limits of tolerance, varying with time and place. Some cultures clearly allow, or even encourage, much greater individual variability than others. And societies likewise differ in their mechanisms of control.

Death has been one of the most usual ways of dealing with dissidents, and imprisonment and torture have also been very popular. In the latter cases the intention has sometimes been not just to destroy but to modify the person, so as to render him an acceptable member of society (or, in the case of the Christian inquisition, of heavenly life after death). The Athenian device of ostracism was one of the more civilized ways of dealing with the problem. The assembly of citizens could vote anonymously to remove an individual from the city for ten years. No disgrace was attached, nor further penalty; it was a way of checking dangerous factions.

Another mechanism of classical Greece (and elsewhere) was that of stigma: a mark, such as a brand, used to mark out permanently those, such as slaves, criminals, and traitors, who were to be shunned and excluded from normal society. Similarly lepers have been forced to ring a bell, and Jews to wear yellow badges. The sociologist Goffman (1963) has used the word stigma to refer to any attribute considered deeply discrediting. Possession of such an attribute – for example handicap, disfigurement, or disabling neurosis – may have distorting effects on personal development (see F2), though it is impossible to make any general rule.

However to some extent such people are inevitably excluded from 'normal' social relationships. An individual may become isolated; he may develop complex techniques for disguising or compensating for his oddity; he may seek normality in the company of others like himself. Sagarin (1969) describes several such groups in *Odd Man In* (e.g. alcoholics and ex-convicts).

Quite often the reaction of society is to encapsulate such individuals in special institutions: hospitals, homes, prisons.

The ensuing secondary effect of institutionalization has often been reported, e.g. by Goffman (1968). It is a complex phenomenon, often arising not so much from malice as from good will combined with necessity. If there are orphans, they must be cared for: it seems more efficient and economical to do so in large homogeneous units. Similarly for the criminal, the old, or the insane. The result tends to be a loss of personal identity, as it has taken modern society some time to realize. Similarly the high-rise flats that have become notorious constituted a well-intentioned effort to clear the slums as quickly and cheaply as might be. Latterly it has been realized that the old terraced property did allow for neighbourliness and a sense of personal possession – 'defensible space' as Hall terms it.

Attempts to reshape the person

Apart from such unfortunate accidents, some societies, or more accurately some groups within particular societies, have set out deliberately to change people. The general aim is to make an individual conform. This can also be one aim of the whole socialization process, and of psychotherapy. Here we must deal with attempts to change the normal adult.

Of course it is relatively simple to produce conformity of behaviour, even without constant pressure (see B1). We conform every time we stop at a red traffic light, partly to avoid accidents and partly from fear of prosecution. Similarly, under suitable circumstances one can alter opinions, or at least expressed opinions. (Stated opinion and behaviour may be contradictory, of course.)

It has been the degraded ambition of some individuals to convert others to their own beliefs in a more fundamental and, they hope, irreversible way. Oddly enough, this often arises from an ostensible desire for the good of the other. It seems to be an unhappy concomitant of believing that one has found the truth, to wish to impose it on others. Unluckily for us, modern technology has now been added to the traditional weapons of conversion.

These attempts have often received fictional expression, the most famous case perhaps being George Orwell's *1984*. With just nine years to go, the politics seem less drastic, but the technology more subtle than Orwell imagined.

Religious conversion, to begin with, stretches back into prehistory. Classic accounts such as that of William James (1901–2), and sensational ones such as those of William Sargant (1957) agree that dramatic conversion rests upon deep-rooted feelings of inadequacy and guilt in the individual. A successful converter, such as John Wesley, Jonathan Edwards, or Billy Graham, uses a selection of dramatic devices to arouse strong emotions in large crowds, doubtless composed, in large part, of those already in a state of conflict. Many classical experiments (such as those of Pavlov, Lashley, etc.) show that the creation of an insoluble conflict results in irrational and ineradicable behaviour. If Freud taught us anything, it is that conscious, reflective rationality is a late and relatively precarious development, easily overturned when emotions are aroused.

It is noteworthy, though, that dramatic conversions alone do not make a movement. Successful proselytizers such as Wesley and Graham commonly set up strong formal organizations to support the beliefs after the charismatic leader has moved on. This is quite consistent with all that we know about group pressures both from observation and from the experiments of such people as Asch, Sherif, and Milgram (see B2).

Religious and political individuals have not hesitated to use every form of violence, when they have been able, against their fellow beings. Sometimes the aim is merely to suppress the dissident, sometimes to change him. Confessions and recantations extracted through torture fill the pages of

Christian history. It is now, however, all but impossible to assess the degree to which the wretched victims of inquisition or witch-hunt came to believe in their own guilt, and to suffer any fundamental change in their individuality. In most cases, the chance of relapse was neatly avoided by execution.

In our own time, the activities of the various totalitarian régimes have become notorious, which is not to say they are unique. Bruno Bettelheim (1960) has given us a prisoner's account of Nazi concentration camps. Everything was done to destroy individuality. Apart from the extreme degradation of living conditions, and the constant presence of violence and the threat of death, prisoners were subject to arbitrary and complete discipline by the guards. The most trivial actions such as going to the toilet – perhaps far from trivial in this context – were controlled. The total effect was to reduce victims to a state of infancy. In extreme cases prisoners seemed to lose their own personality and begin to model themselves upon that of the guards, aping their mannerisms and dress.

An excellent but rather neglected film, *The Prisoner*, showed some of the ways in which political confessions can be extracted. Many reports give combinations of the same methods. The subject is generally taken suddenly from his own environment and put in solitary confinement. Poor and little food and prolonged deprivation of sleep reduce his physical strength and his sense of reality. He is allowed no possessions and only ill-fitting clothes. He is addressed by a number, but must give his captors their full titles. Incessant interrogation is designed not just to force an admission of guilt but to cause the prisoner to feel guilty, building on his loss of reality, confusion, and fear. An intolerable situation is created from which escape is possible by compliance with those in authority – who then at once become lenient and accepting. They are, however, skilful at detecting deceit.

We are now in the realms of so-called 'brain-washing' (a translation of the Chinese *hsi nao*, 'wash brain'), or more euphemistically 'thought reform'. This was practised on prisoners of war in Korea, and on 'reactionaries' in Communist China. In the first case it appears that, although the treatment of prisoners fell far below the standards of the Geneva convention, they were not subjected to systematic violence so much as intensive indoctrination. This worked best with individuals who were already discontented with their own society, and who lacked the support of a strong organization (another film, *Bridge on the River Kwai*, showed quite convincingly the supportive nature of good discipline). Even without this, relatively few individuals could be said to be 'converted': of a total of 7,190 US prisoners, twenty-one decided not to return home, and some of these doubtless had communist leanings beforehand. On the other hand 2,730 died in captivity, and one out of every three engaged in some form of collaboration. Some of the other forces, for example the Turks, showed very much smaller figures: for example in one camp where 400–800 Americans out of 1,500–1,800 died, none of the 110 Turks died (Brown, 1963).

The more complete and drastic Chinese programme was studied by Lifton (1961). It was applied both to Chinese citizens and to foreigners, and from some of the latter Lifton was able to obtain vivid first-hand accounts when they had returned to the West. The most basic feature seems to be total control of human communication: 'milieu control'. The entire social environment in which the individual finds himself is directed to one end: his conversion to the truth. An individual is not just imprisoned, he is surrounded night and day with the already converted, dedicated to his salvation. As in the other programmes, physical means are used for three main purposes. First to lessen resistance; second to attack the attributes of individuality and reduce the victim to a state of infancy-like confusion and dependence; third to punish the prisoner whenever he deviates from what is required. Indeed it is not just a matter of enforcing particular

105

behaviour, but of insistently demanding ever further steps along the true road. The psychological techniques used resemble those familiar both from folklore and from psychological studies. They include confusion; induction of shame and guilt; public confession; successive increase of demands; persistent exhortation and 'help'; restriction of concepts through language manipulation. (The last was developed by Orwell as 'newspeak'.)

Such techniques can, it seems, be effective, at least as long as milieu control is maintained. Individuals do seem to be genuinely 'converted'. It is not just that they now obediently express a certain set of opinions. Rather, it is that thought now proceeds upon a different set of assumptions, which are rigid and resistant to change. The individual has become less master of himself, his perception of reality more distorted. According to Lifton, the actual acceptance of the new views may be most dramatic in those individuals who have always thought in a stereotyped way. It also seems that on removal from the controlled environment the individual may slowly, and with difficulty, revert to 'normal'. The removal of the supports, dependence on which has been systematically induced, may be traumatic. In many ways, freedom is harder than slavery.

J. A. C. Brown concludes, as many others have done, first that there is little new in the twentieth century attempts to control men's minds, and second that whatever such attempts may be, there will always be those who will resist. I (JR) think this far too optimistic. First there are already, or in all likelihood will shortly be, more powerful techniques of control than have ever existed. It is very difficult to see how any individual could possibly prevail against a developed genetic engineering or electrode implantation. It may be said, that no-one could implant electrodes in the population of the world: but this is, at best, a practical difficulty, not one of principle. It is not a mere fantasy to imagine, say, a small colony on the moon, with the world's population destroyed.

Then take the matter of milieu control. It seems likely that China today is doing this more effectively than ever before. I fear that there may be a point of no return beyond which 'the people's will' may be irreversible. I fear the replacement of reason by dogma, and of autonomy by obedience. Much of this was achieved over a period of centuries by the medieval Church, with not a fraction of today's technical means of control.

Master and disciple

One of the oldest and most universal ways in which one individual is influenced by another is through the relationship of master and disciple, to give it a generic title. Whether this results in destruction or enhancement of the person is a matter for debate.

By this relationship we mean all those cases where one individual regularly reports to another, generally in a position of authority. It is likely that, if two strangers were put in such a situation daily, within a fairly short time some degree of emotion would develop. More usually this is there from the start, indeed it is part of the reason for the arrangement. The context may be one of religion, education, or therapy. The mechanism of confession has been one of the great strengths of the Roman Church for many hundreds of years. In several Eastern religions the attachment of a disciple – *chela* – to a master – *guru* – has long been basic to the system of instruction. This method has become rather well known with the recent popularization of one master after another in the West, and the searches for truth of famous pop stars. For a more objective account, see *Godmen of India* by Peter Brent (1972); and for a revealing though fictional version, *Kim*, by Rudyard Kipling.

The mechanism has been most systematically refined in Zen Buddhism. Zen has become extensively known in the

West in a 'hippie' or 'beatnik' context, where it seems, often, to be a synonym for 'do your own thing'. Nothing could be further from the truth. Zen, as traditionally practised in Japan, is a series of spiritual exercises designed to produce, if successful, the state of 'enlightenment'. Hard to specify exactly, this seems to involve a heightened awareness of reality, a sense of the oneness of creation, and other benefits. Whatever the state that is sought or achieved, it is sufficient to influence dramatically the lives of many individuals. There are different paths to enlightenment, but several of them involve the intensive practice of a strict discipline. Let us mention two. In one approach, the aspirant is posed an insoluble problem (*koan*) by the master, for example: What is the sound of one hand clapping? In the course of a regular programme of work, eating, sleeping, and meditation, the novice visits the master several times a day to offer his solution. Since the problem is intellectually insoluble, the solution is always inadequate, and the novice's effort may be met by tart replies, silence, or blows. In this way a state of intense anxiety and conflict is created, which if conditions are right is eventually resolved in an emotional crisis producing enlightenment.

In another procedure, training in one of the various traditional skills is made the vehicle of spiritual development – archery, swordsmanship, calligraphy, flower arranging, etc. Again discipline under a master is severe and prolonged, concentrating on the exact performance of each component of the skill until, as is common with skills, they become automatic.

There is no doubt at all that these procedures bring about marked changes in personality. But there is much doubt as to the nature of the changes. Some hold that the individual becomes more free and independent, others that the student incorporates the value system of the master thus being, while doubtless more certain and confident, less autonomous.

We can at least see some of the resemblances to confession

and to thought reform. The Oxbridge tutorial system, well known to produce changes in personality, similarly involves the student in a regular meeting with his superior, a tutor, to whom he presents his (often) best efforts. Anecdote tells us that this too can be a situation of conflict and anxiety, with lasting effects beyond the merely intellectual.

In terms of psychoanalysis, what happens in such situations is transference. Basic to psychoanalytic theory is the assumption that every relationship tends to reactivate the emotional patterns laid down in early childhood. The more intense the relationship, the more the unresolved conflicts of the original parent-infant situation will be reproduced. In psychoanalytic therapy, this is done deliberately: or rather, the analyst knows it must happen, and concentrates on demonstrating this to the patient, so as to make him aware of his own feelings and thus enabling him to work through the conflicts and resolve them in a mature and realistic way. That at least is the theory. And the theory would correspondingly explain the changes brought about for political, religious, or educational ends as involving the same basic mechanism.

There are at least two important comments to be made. First there is the problem of what value this 'explanation' has. We have already mentioned some of the problems of psychoanalysis as a scientific theory. It is certainly not clear that another psychological theory might not turn out to be better in the long run: but at present, one can at least say that the alternatives – such as conditioning – seem even less plausible. It is worth pausing briefly to explain 'conditioning' (see A3).

Perhaps the most sweeping claims were made by J. B. Watson, who claimed that given a young child and a free hand he could produce any sort of adult to order. This was never put to the test, and Watson's claim rested largely on his success in conditioning a small child, Albert, to be afraid of a woolly rabbit, by pairing its appearance with a loud and frightening noise. This was a strict application of Pavlov's procedure, and so properly called 'conditioning'. The word is often misused to mean something like 'accustomed to' or 'influenced by': – 'we are all conditioned by the mass media'. This mechanism was given fictional status by Aldous Huxley in *Brave New World*.

Another correct use applies to *operant conditioning*, a behaviouristic method developed by B. F. Skinner. Essentially, this seeks to account for all behaviour by showing how each action is *reinforced* by some stimulus that increases the probability of the response. Skinnerian methods are undoubtedly extremely efficient with a range of animal behaviour, and have been applied to at least some human behaviour. For example withdrawn psychiatric patients can be brought to be socially interactive. Programmed instruction, in which each correct answer is immediately rewarded, is derived from operant principles. Skinner has claimed that very complex behaviour like language follows the same pattern. Indeed, more fancifully, he has envisaged in his novel, *Walden Two*, a whole community based upon operant conditioning. In *Beyond Freedom and Dignity* he seems to see conditioning as the way forward for the human race. Probably few other psychologists agree. There are logical and empirical reasons to think that the application of the method is limited.

Then again, a religious or otherwise committed person might claim that psychoanalysis, far from explaining, is but a weak imitation of *his* system. There is at present no way of deciding between such claims, for the reasons given in Chapter 1. What we can say is that we have a number of phenomena that *seem* to have something in common; and that the 'reactivation' concept does seem, in some degree, to correspond to an experience that many people have. In intense personal relationships we do seem, often, to be repeating earlier experiences, which subjectively seem convincingly like those of very early childhood.

The second point concerns the outcome of these experiences. As Mae West once remarked when, temporarily standing in for the local schoolteacher, she noticed the day's writing lesson on the blackboard: 'I am a good girl; I am a good boy; I am a good man. What is this – propaganda?'

What, if anything, is the difference between education and propaganda, or between therapy and indoctrination? In line with what we have already said, we believe the distinction must lie in whether or not the individual, as a result of the process, is more able to act rationally, autonomously, and in relation to reality. This is easy to say, but very hard to establish in practice. There is first the intractable problem of what reality is; but from a common sense point of view we can generally rely on effects (for example, the falsity of a belief that one can fly is shown by falling to the ground); backed up, though not very reliably, by general opinion. (The trouble with the latter is that it has often turned out to be wrong, e.g. the view that the earth was flat.)

Then, next, it is very hard to show, in a particular case, whether an action is done rationally or irrationally. This is aggravated, third, by the subjective feeling of freedom that may accompany an irrational conviction. Indeed this is often made an article of faith: true freedom, it is said, is found in obedience to some law (usually God's). This approaches Orwell's 'newspeak'. Often, of course, acceptance of a set of beliefs does produce a *sort* of freedom: freedom from anxiety, from the need to make decisions. But this, we suggest, diminishes rather than enhances our human status.

It seems clear that political ideological programmes are intended to reduce individual autonomy, and to a greater or lesser extent succeed. How far educational and religious programmes do this, each person must decide. Let us say a little more about some forms of psychological therapy (see F3).

'Therapy' is defined by the dictionary as 'medical treatment'. This is rather misleading, since the medical approach is only one way of looking at illness (see F1). Somewhat confusingly, a parallel term 'psychotherapy' has come to mean, roughly, 'treatment by non-physical means'. In fact, medicine is not confined to physical means, nor psychology to the non-physical. In fact, given a particular complaint, it is often (perhaps always) unwise to isolate physical, social, and individual aspects.

There is, however, a difference in approach. Very approximately, what may be distinguished as a 'medical' approach supposes that a person who comes for help is, so to speak, normal but with something wrong, like chickenpox or a broken leg. Isolate the cause, remove it, and the patient is cured. Similarly, someone who is severely depressed, perhaps to the point of suicide, 'has' a depression. Even though we cannot isolate a physical cause, we know that the symptoms can often be relieved by drugs, electric shock, or surgery. These, therefore, are commonly applied.

In contrast a 'sociological' approach tends to argue that it is the individual's social environment, perhaps society as a whole, that is at fault. Psychotic persons are reacting understandably to intolerable situations; those who are depressed have reason to be. While there is undoubtedly some truth in this, it is only part of the story (see above).

A 'psychological' approach *should* centre on the individual: his physical makeup, his circumstances, and his unique adjustment.

A lot of disagreement over methods of therapy stems from confusion over aims. On the 'medical' model, a patient is cured when the symptoms disappear. The 'sociological' view tends to reject the notion of cure along with that of illness, but may seek to construct a social group within which the individual can function. *Some* 'psychological' approaches seek not just to cure but actually to enhance the person's capabilities.

Thus what is known as behaviour therapy tends to adopt the medical pattern. A distressing trait such as fear of open spaces, or crowds, it is argued, has been learned, and can therefore be unlearned and replaced by normal behaviour. When this is done, the patient is cured. The methods of Alcoholics Anonymous and similar groups show features of the sociological approach. The alcoholic is not 'cured' but adopts a non-drinking life-style within a supportive social group. Psychoanalytic therapy stresses not so much a return to normal functioning as a full resolution of the underlying conflicts which are common to all, but which in some individuals break out, so to speak, in symptoms. In theory, the patient after successful analysis is *better* adjusted than he who has never had occasion for treatment. This aspect has been developed further in the work of C. G. Jung, whose often middle-aged patients sought not just relief from symptoms, but some increased sense of self-identity or meaning in life.

Now to the extent that a particular symptom inhibits an individual's ability to act autonomously, removal of the symptom must enhance it. Thus if, for example, one can learn not to be pathologically afraid of crowds, one has the choice of joining a group where before one did not. If one can be relieved of obsessive thoughts of suicide, the possibility of a more productive way of life opens up. Two objections are often made to this line of argument. The psychoanalytic objection is that only the symptoms, not the underlying conflict, has been removed, so that illness will recur. Insofar as this has been tested, there seems to be little evidence to support it (see D3).

- The second objection is that the actual means of treatment itself reduces the individual's capacity for self-determination. An extreme case of this would be surgery (pre-frontal

113

lobotomy) which may relieve depression but only at the cost of loss of part of the brain, and consequently probably of ability to plan, etc. Similarly, however, it may be argued that drugs reduce the capacity for reality-oriented decision-making. Behaviour therapy merely substitutes one habit for another.

It is not just that such effects may *follow* from the therapy: the argument is that they are implicit in it, since the therapy is something *done to* the patient. The individual is reduced to an object by the actual treatment and by the whole institutional context in which treatment is carried out. The latter is now recognized as a real danger in at least some institutions: and some hospitals, at least, attempt to treat the patient rather than the illness.

The problem remains as to whether therapy enhances or diminishes the person: and with regard to psychoanalysis in particular it is difficult to see how to reach a firm conclusion. The test would seem to lie in the individual's ability to respond to reason and reality. Freud claimed: 'Where id was, there shall ego be'; but, as far as we know, no one has yet submitted this to a real empirical test.

The same arguments must apply to education and to religious systems. If their aim is really to increase individual autonomy and genuine freedom, then the *principle* of testing is quite clear. The practical problems are great. Of course, many might claim that the object of education, religion, and even therapy is *not* to increase autonomy, but to instil particular views and doctrines. Such a view we think profoundly mistaken.

Survival

An encouraging human trait is the capacity for survival under the most adverse conditions. And not just physical survival, but the preservation of human qualities. This has been seen throughout recorded history in cases of imprisonment, torture, and death when individuals have resisted every attempt to make them betray their ideals or to crush their resistance. Saint-Exupéry tells of an airman who, having crashed in a remote South American jungle, at last against all the odds found his way back to civilization. He said: 'I have done what no animal could do.' Similarly in conditions of extreme disorder, such as war and post-war chaos, famine and other disasters, individuals frequently do not merely survive, but call forth unexpected reserves of courage and humanity.

The history of the village of Eyam in Derbyshire is famous. In the plague year of 1665 the villagers deliberately refused to fly for safety, so as to avoid carrying the disease elsewhere. *The Diary of Anne Frank* is likewise a famous account of one individual's development under terrible conditions. (Allport, Bruner, and Jandorf, 1941, collated ninety life-histories of persons under Nazi rule which give many interesting comparisons.)

Such examples have led to the supposition that the human spirit is unconquerable, that freedom and independence will always survive and eventually triumph. Unfortunately this seems to be merely a comforting article of faith. As has already been said, there seems no reason in principle why an increase in the technological means of control should not reach a point of no return.

The opposing views have been put in fictional form in Orwell's *1984* and David Karp's *One*. In the latter story an individual resists all the attempts of a powerful state to destroy his individuality. Orwell's hero, Winston Smith, on the other hand, finally succumbs: he loved Big Brother. Orwell, we fear, had the truer vision.

RK: Well, you say 'we' quite confidently, but I'm not at all sure I agree. You could just as well argue that the human potential movement will produce an irreversible change

115

the other way – a world in which everyone is reaching personal fulfilment, and feels no need to tyrannize over anyone else.

JR: Perhaps logically that is so. I admit my view may well be based as much on temperament as on evidence. I have this Anglo-Saxon streak, a sort of defiant pessimism. Fate will win in the end, but one can at least resist as long as possible. Read *The Battle of Maldon* – I won't quote it here as I don't suppose the typesetters have any Anglo-Saxon characters.

RK: All right, you needn't parade your scholarship. Instead, let's turn to the positive side – only you're bound to give a biased account.

JR: All accounts are biased. And I'll let you get a few words in.

6
Can the person be enhanced?

Throughout recorded history there have been those who have sought to make themselves or others 'better': not necessarily stronger, richer, or more powerful, but in some way more developed as persons. *Some* of these attempts seem related to the sort of characteristics we gave in the last chapter – identity, autonomy, grasp of reality. Possibly all of them are, though one of us (JR) thinks that very unlikely.

At the same time probably everyone can recognize among his own acquaintances, or among distinguished persons, some who seem to have more than the average of such charactersistics.

If this is so, it seems that the answer to the title question must be yes. But, of course, it is not so simple. There is first the problem of trying to see whether there is any sort of general agreement over concepts. There is the problem of other issues – moral, religious, political, historical – intruding with confusion. And there is the vast and hardly attempted task of sorting out the plethora of methods.

Many programmes of improvement have developed in a religious or philosophical context. We wish, if possible, to emphasize the psychological aspects.

117

What a psychologist would wish to do is to establish some facts: in what ways, and how, can persons be 'enhanced'? Now if you want to know something about a person, the first and most obvious step is to ask him. In their search for objectivity psychologists tended to despise this method during the dominance of Behaviourism (roughly, 1920–1960). However such introspective evidence is more useful for some things than for others. The most useful first evidence about what a person feels or wants is what he says he feels or wants. It is not all the evidence, for he may be lying or ill. It is less good for what he actually does do, and still less good on the value of what he does. Artists are notoriously poor assessors of their own work. Eysenck has reported that 90 per cent of people in general think they have a better than average sense of humour.

Further, we know from the work of Leon Festinger that there is a very general tendency to adjust one's accomplishments and goals to fit each other – to reduce 'cognitive dissonance' (see B3). Thus the car we actually bought becomes better than the one we rejected. The religion, or politics, or therapy, or self-development programme, in which we have invested time and money, has to be good value. Even further, of course, this belief may itself *make* the activity more effective, when something as intangible as personality change is in question.

Thus it will be an interesting fact if people feel themselves to be more independent, or happier, or what not, after certain experiences than before; but it will not necessarily correspond to reality. We should like to know, at least, if *other* people think they have changed for the better. And we should like to know, even more, if their observable behaviour reflects any such change. Such evidence is remarkably hard to come by.

RK: Not surprisingly, as we have yet to do the preliminary conceptual and empirical work on the improvement of mankind through 'human potential' techniques. And we never will have the data, if you have your way.

JR: Most unfair, since what I ask for is precisely some proper investigation to replace the present combination of confused faith and commercial exploitation.

Self-actualization

Following the domination of Behaviourism, a reaction set in, led by those who were interested in experience, in personal development, in human values in Psychology. The movement came to be known as humanistic psychology. It also came to be known as 'third force' psychology (the other being psychoanalysis). Both these terms are vague, and different writers claim and disclaim the titles. Of many figures, perhaps the leader was Abraham Maslow. It was he who called for a 'third force', and it was he who popularized the term 'self-actualization', which he borrowed from Kurt Goldstein, as a concept of personal development. Maslow was originally struck with admiration for two people who taught him – the anthropologist, Ruth Benedict, and the psychologist, Max Wertheimer – and wished to understand their personalities and see if there were any more like them.

The concept of self-actualization derives partly from Henry Murray's theory of needs. This holds that human behaviour is based on needs which are arranged in a hierarchy: that is to say, there are those (such as for food and shelter) which are more basic, and which must be satisfied before attention can be paid to those (such as for love or aesthetic satisfaction) which are higher in the scale. It isn't much of a theory since there is little evidence for it and since it conflicts with common sense. (It is not uncommon to put beauty or learning even before food, sleep, or sex.) However at least it is reasonably clear, which is more than can be said for Maslow.

In Maslow's theory, the highest need is for self-actualization. Maslow describes this need in many words, and often seems to think that he has given objective criteria in terms of behaviour. For example in 1967 he offered eight 'ways in which one self-actualizes'. These seem to be as follows: experiencing fully; making conscious choices; making 'growth' choices; being honest; being prepared to be unpopular or different; working hard at something one wants to do; finding out what one is like; having 'peak experiences'. This last, another Maslow phrase, refers to something like ecstacy or insight (themselves vague words).

Now the trouble with this sort of approach is not that there may not be much truth in it. Indeed the humanistic writers have done Psychology a great service in reasserting the importance of individual experience and of human values. The trouble is that so far the approach has failed to lead on anywhere further. 'Humanistic' psychology books have sold extremely widely, largely one suspects because they are full of nice comforting uplifting thoughts. But the thoughts remain the personal intuition of the writers. They may be morally and ethically desirable, but are they psychologically sound? If not, they are only a version of what the great religions have offered much more systematically and convincingly.

Take the eight ways of self-actualizing above: there is really no evidence at all that these are related to each other, that they produce a specifiable result, or that they have specific causes.

RK: This seems less than fair to Maslow. The achievement of Maslow and his colleagues is severalfold. First they have raised the important question of the criteria for positive mental health. They have made suggestions for answers, drawn from Maslow's studies of exceptionally healthy people, of whom his teachers were only two. Maslow (1934) reported that these people, whom he called 'self-actualizers', shared a number of characteristics, such as greater perceptual flexibility, ego strength, tolerance, humour, creativity, tendency to have peak experiences, etc. This is at least a start. Then there is the subsequent assertion by Maslovians that all humans have potential for this degree of mental health. Hence the 'human potential' movement. The many techniques they have devised are preliminary steps towards actualizing that potential.

This is by no means the limit of Maslow's contribution. He also made a valuable distinction between two kinds of motives: D (Deficiency) and B (Being) motives. The former include obvious tissue deficits such as hunger, which motivates all animals; the latter are essentially human – they are motives for personal growth and expansion, and they are more common in self-actualizing individuals. I also think it unfair to show that Maslow's usages of the term self-actualization were inconsistent. He was trying to explore the parameters and the connotations of words pertaining to the enhancement of persons. He deserves our sympathy.

Techniques for growth

We had better touch briefly on some of the many techniques that have been supposed to enhance the person. There are in all probability many thousands of these, and to the best of our knowledge no-one has ever attempted a systematic classification, still less analysis. Our grouping is mainly in terms of the context within which the techniques are practised.

We have already mentioned therapy. In Freudian theory, the fully developed person is the completely analysed one: one no longer controlled by unconscious conflicts and anxieties created during the traumata of infancy. C. G. Jung, originally Freud's disciple, took several steps away from this with his concept of *individuation*. The process of individuation certainly involves becoming free from neurotic conflicts, but also the integration of different aspects of the personality. One of the ways in which Jung differed from Freud was in his assumption that each of us in some sense contains all the aspects of a complete person. In any individual, some aspects are dominant, the other, opposite aspects are not. Thus an extreme extravert is one in which the extraverted traits are dominant, overt, and conscious. Introverted traits are repressed and hidden. Individuation would involve the integration of both aspects into one well rounded personality. This is achieved through Jungian analysis, but may also come about, in Jung's view, almost spontaneously, or through various traditional religious and magical practices. Jung considered, for example, that alchemists were not – or not merely – involved in pseudo-chemistry, but were really concerned with exploring and integrating their own unconscious mental processes.

This view is supported by, for example, the work of Mircea Eliade (1964) and Frances Yates (1964) who have shown how dominant the aim of some form of personal or spiritual development has been in most occult systems. Indeed for many centuries it was not possible to separate the occult from the practical, so that (for example) the trade of a smith was an indissoluble blend of technology and spirituality. This is found throughout world folklore, but is seen most explicitly in the Japanese swordsmith. Whether our present view constitutes an advance, each person must decide.

It seems clear that the theories of Freud and Jung are quite inconsistent with each other and with that of Maslow. And the same thing applies to a host of other theories. My opinion (JR) for what it is worth is that very many people have stumbled over one or more of a group of probably related phenomena, and have formulated very various theories in an attempt to make sense of what they found. The phenomena are real enough, and call for an explanation; but as yet there seem no convincing grounds for preferring one explanation to another.

Even more than to therapy, this applies to the currently popular programmes for self-development. Often described as radically new, or sometimes as a rediscovery of old ideas, these appear often to be a jumble of half-understood scraps picked up from here, there, and everywhere. To support a general condemnation we should need an exhaustive review, which is not possible. Let us give as one example the methods of Oscar Ichazo as described by John Lilly (*The Centre of the Cyclone*, 1972). The system is now commercially available under the name of *Arica*.

John Lilly has investigated many unusual phenomena, such as the effects of drugs and of sensory deprivation, with the aim of gaining personal development. Ichazo's system appears to be a new combination of elements drawn from several others. It was carried out at a place (Arica) in Chile which is relatively isolated and some 3,000 feet above sea level. (It has often been suggested that the popularity of mountain tops for meditation is due to the psychological effects of a degree of oxygen deprivation, e.g. hallucinations.)

One main method was physical exercises, drawn from yoga, *aikido* (a Japanese system), and the American Air Force. Another part was meditation and prayer, often in an isolation somewhat resembling that of monks in a cloister, i.e. standing or walking alone with a hood drawn over the face. An unusual practice combined these by running up and down hills, sometimes carrying large rocks, the movement being accompanied by a kind of dedicatory meditation. Such relatively violent methods may have a parallel in, for example, the people of Pentecost Island (New Hebrides) who, for religious reasons, throw themselves from the top of tall platforms, being arrested a few inches from the ground by a rope tied to the ankle. Another part of the system was teaching and discussion from Oscar Ichazo himself.

As to the results, Lilly is extremely vague, except for indicating he found the experiences valuable. He does give in some detail however a sort of theoretical analysis, which seems to derive largely from the work of George Gurdjieff (1877–1949), a Russian mystic. It consists in a description of 'states of consciousness' or 'vibration levels'. (Gurdjieff's notion seems to have been that the matter of which the universe is composed varies in density and in 'vibrations' – the more dense, the fewer the vibrations. Spiritual advancement involves attainment of higher levels of vibration.) This analysis is linked to astrology, the precise moment of birth determining the individual's capacities and life style. Becoming aware of such predispositions is important if one wishes to attain the higher levels of consciousness.

The scientifically inclined reader may be disposed to reject all this as preposterous. It is only fair to Lilly to stress that his method is to accept a new theory *as if* it were true, in order to see what use can be made of it. He says that this particular theory led him to look at certain ideas in a new way: 'This does not prove its "truth"; it shows only its didactic usefulness'.

The theories of Oscar Ichazo may or may not seem to be nonsense. So may those of a thousand other systems. What is undeniable is that throughout recorded history the lives of millions of persons have been profoundly influenced, not to say dominated, by such systems of belief and programmes of action. So far, Psychology has almost completely ignored such clearly important psychological phenomena.

Indeed it may sometimes be hard to recognize that phenomena *are* psychological, because other aspects tend to be dominant. This may be so, for example, in a religious context, perhaps especially a Christian one. For many, religious observance has become little more than a convention. For others, questions of theology, quite understandably, are of the first importance. For a psychologist, at least two aspects ought to be of the greatest interest. One is the motivational role of religious belief and practice; the other, more relevant here, is the nature of religious experience. The great mystics of Christianity (and other religions) have sought to achieve a 'psychological' state described in some such phrase as 'unity with God'. Whatever the particular doctrinal context, this state is commonly said to be essentially inexpressible in words, but to involve feelings of joy and certainty and a conviction of being in direct contact with reality – sometimes, with 'another' reality felt to be *more* real than the everyday one.

Now cognitive psychologists, whatever else they may disagree on, agree on one thing, that the direct experience of reality is impossible (see A1). Freud, the Gestalt school, Piaget, the Harvard school led by J. S. Bruner, the British line of workers such as Bartlett, Craik, and Gregory – are all unanimous. What we experience is a constructed model of reality. There would probably also be general agreement that in the course of individual development this model or representation passes through a number of stages (see C2). The earliest stage is closely linked to action: an infant reacts to stimuli, it cannot control or manipulate – think about – its environment symbolically. The next stage is linked to imagery, and the third to symbolic processes, of which language is by far the most powerful. (These very complex concepts are discussed in detail in *Thinking: Its Nature and Development* by Radford and Burton, 1974.)

It seems plausible to suggest that mystical experience corresponds in some sense to an early stage of development, before words become available and when the individual may well feel himself to be at one with the rest of creation, not yet a distinct individual. This sort of explanation was indeed proposed by Freud. If it is true then the achievements of mystics can hardly be said to constitute progress. In important respects they represent the opposite of maturity.

125

RK: This is an absurd conclusion. Presumably you would not wish to say that falling in love was also regressive, nor the experience of aesthetic merit an indication of immaturity, nor the actions of altruism an index of second childhood. Yet mystical experiences are only an extension of these experiences, which are widely regarded as the pinnacle of human conscious endeavour.

JR: I should think most people might agree that falling in love *is* regressive in some ways at least. And as before you are content with assertions in place of argument.

RK: Moreover you seem to have too simple a view of reality. Without entering metaphysical complexities I would, at the very least, put before the reader the possibility, brilliantly expounded by William James (1902) in *The Varieties of Religious Experience*, that in religious experience persons come into contact with a different type of reality, one which they know directly. Indeed Buddhists and Hindus claim that man has a special cognitive faculty, *Buddhi*, with which 'reality' may be directly apprehended. This undercuts your objection about constructed models of reality.

JR: It's an alternative hypothesis. Personally I think that argument and evidence are against it.

The case that the mystical claims are true has been well presented many times, e.g. by Evelyn Underhill (1961). It is too far from our main theme to argue here. A difficulty is that it seems one is often faced with the alternatives of accepting the convictions of those who have had certain experiences on the strength of their reports, or rejecting altogether the value of what they say. Another tentative hypothesis is that one could regard the construction of a model of reality as analogous to the acquisition of a skill. Indeed it has been argued that the control of skilled performances does depend upon such internal models (Gregory, 1970). If some kind of skill were improved sufficiently, it might be almost equivalent to direct perception. One can compare the almost instantaneous reactions of a master games player. We have already mentioned the use of skills training to bring about enlightenment in Zen Buddhism. It is interesting that sportsmen do speak of an almost ecstatic quality accompanying peak performances (e.g. Tony Jacklin in *The Sunday Times*, 4 November 1973). We may also note that over-mastered skills can generally not be expressed in language: they are 'unconscious'. Indeed the attempt to express them verbally tends to make them break down.

However this may be, the methods of many mystics do seem to have some things in common, such as isolation, concentration, repetition of some phrase or act, deprivation (e.g. of food or oxygen; sensory deprivation). It is not to be expected that methods will be uniform, since they must arise also from doctrine, tradition, or idiosyncrasy.

The experiences of mystics, or even of sportsmen, have been little studied by experimental psychologists. They have spent much time, however, on creative thinking, though without reaching any very definite conclusions (see A7). One of the more reliable findings is that really creative thought involves a high level of dedication of time and energy: great achievements commonly demand all that the individual can give, at least for the moment. Another general result is that geniuses cannot report on the origin of their conceptions. *Something* happens outside of conscious awareness. This is true of scientists as well as artists, and even, for example, of chess masters (De Groot, 1965). Here perhaps we can see that while an individual who acts in accordance with reality is one who acts consciously, at the same time there is a sense in which full development requires an exploration of parts of the person which are normally hidden.

Of course this is not to say that highly creative people are necessarily more autonomous than others except in their own field. There, it is common to regard as a genius one who has the independence to break the accepted rules. In private life, as it were, the highly creative may show every variety of personality. Anecdotes of genius could be made to support either Freud's notion of sublimation or Maslow's of self-actualization; and still more would fit neither pattern.

Insufficient attention has been paid to the role of knowledge and skill in the growth of the person. Clearly in a quite practical sense the acquisition of a range of skills makes an individual more independent, until he becomes virtually self-sufficient like Robinson Crusoe or Henry Thoreau. (Compare *Fat of the Land* by John Seymour, 1961.) Similarly it seems undeniable that awareness of more of human knowledge constitutes a dimension of personal development. Of course there can be scholars whose lives are restricted to an arid scholarship, but the current tendency is to devalue learning in favour of feeling. Correspondingly in attempts to increase creativity the trend has been to stress spontaneity to the neglect of technique and discipline. Yet what we know of both individual and historical development suggests (to me, JR) that creativity *arises out of* techniques and knowledge. Art by rule alone is generally sterile, but inspiration alone is too often vapid and trivial. The trick, which no one has yet mastered, is to contrive the best balance between them. 'Creativity training' has flourished very profitably for some years. A search of the published literature fails to reveal many results of unquestionable value. However it must be admitted that we lack agreed criteria for improvement in creativity, or even as to what constitutes creativity.

The current passion for the spontaneous, the free, and the formless is understandable as a reaction against the clearly disastrous results of science and technology. Somehow or other the promise of progress through scientific knowledge towards an ideal, peaceful, and amply provided society has been betrayed. It is now a commonplace to remark that wars have become more frightful than ever before, that our society has largely lost any sense of human values, and that we are well on the way to the complete exhaustion or pol-

128

lution of all natural resources. One answer is to try to create an alternative society beside or within the existing one. We must discuss this shortly.

Another (closely related) is to seek individual freedom through traditional – and some new – techniques, of which drugs and magic in particular have become rather popular. The use of drugs for psychological purposes is of course extremely ancient, although a few new items such as LSD have lately been added to the pharmacopoeia. Traditionally, drugs have been used to release and enliven; and more dramatically, to allow of spiritual experiences not attainable in the ordinary state. Many individuals, including such a pragmatic philosopher as William James, have claimed that the use of drugs reveals to them the sense of realities previously unguessed at. Such experiences can be compared with the classical spirit journey of the *shaman* – he who sees – found in almost every non-technological society. Even the wretched witches tortured and burnt at the beginning of our modern period in Europe are known to have included psychedelic agents in their brews and ointments (Harner, 1973). Today 'taking a trip' refers to the less structured adventures of those who emphasize their protest by the use of substances condemned as illegal by the properly constituted authorities. It is noteworthy that the non-illegal materials (nutmeg, for example) are far less popular. Wells (1973) points out that the effects obtained depend heavily upon setting and expectations.

At least since the romantic opium eating of Coleridge and De Quincey it has been claimed that creative faculties can be released by drugs. Perhaps they can: but there is little evidence of their general efficacy. Nor for their general usefulness in attaining personal development, at least in terms of our criteria. In a given case, perhaps, drugs may help an individual to accept hitherto unacceptable aspects of his own personality. But in my view (JR) the general effect of drugs must be to distort the processes of full mental functioning,

129

those that help to make us fully human.

Dying of inoperable cancer, Freud, the great realist, refused all pain-relieving drugs. He said: 'I prefer to think in torment than not to be able to think clearly'.

The apparent inability of science to produce an ideal, or even a tolerable, society has no doubt contributed to the current resurgence of interest in the occult and the magical. Contests between science and magic have occurred before: in the sixth and fifth centuries BC, first and second centuries AD, and at the Renaissance. Science won the first and third and lost or drew the second. Magic is closely related to personal development in several ways. Quite simply and practically, many magical practices help people to make up their minds; or, perhaps, to realize what they have already decided. This is very often the real purpose of visiting a fortune teller or soothsayer (= truth teller); or indeed a physician or psychologist (Thomas, 1971).

At a more sophisticated level, one function of magical rituals is often said to be the determination of one's 'true will' or the like. It has been said that everything which a person does with intention is a truly magical rite. This was the aim of probably the most famous of modern magicians, Aleister Crowley. The true will is probably fairly closely related to becoming aware of one's unconscious desires, and magical rituals (in the traditions followed by Crowley, and several other traditions also) are designed to create states of high emotional tension and release. The effects must in some ways be analogous to those of therapy. However the underlying assumptions are almost opposite. The magician believes that in his moments of ecstasy he achieves power to bring about changes by the action of his will. Psychoanalysis, at least, would consider this a regression to the level of an infantile belief in the omnipotence of thought. Crowley believed he had become, first a saint, then a god. Like some other incarnate gods, his powers did not prevent him dying rather sadly, almost alone and forgotten.

130

There is yet a further aspect to magic. Some of the most powerful traditions (e.g. that on which *I Ching* is based, and the Western hermetic and cabbalistic traditions) suppose, in contrast to science, that the universe is essentially orderly, and all of a piece, so that a change in any part affects all other parts. This is the fundamental assumption of astrology: 'as above, so below'. Thus the road to self-determination is through awareness of the forces acting upon us, and the effects of our actions on the world. It is for this reason that the *I Ching* – widely available in paperback form – promises not merely to foretell the future, but growth in personal development.

Whatever the scientifically inclined may think of such notions, it is useless to deny their great appeal. Indeed if one were to consider all the human beings that have ever lived, it is almost certain that by far the greatest number have lived – perhaps even still live – in accordance with systems of thought that are 'magical' rather than 'scientific'.

Above all, perhaps, those who have sought personal development of some kind have done so in a mystical or magical context. Many scholars (e.g. Eliade, 1963) have pointed to the well-nigh universal occurrence of fundamental patterns of behaviour and experience, such as that of death and rebirth. Widely scattered traditions, such as those of shamanism, alchemy, and mystery religions (all with many varied exemplars) have deliberately practised techniques designed to bring about some kind of 'death' or return to a primordial state of undifferentiated being, the necessary prelude to the birth of the enlightened initiate. Those familiar with the folk traditions of Western Europe will promptly see parallels (the Marshfield Paper Boys, a traditional Gloucestershire mummers' troupe, come to mind). And a most obvious analogy is with the process of psychoanalysis.

Yet another facet of the reaction against technology has been the interest in 'experience'. This is closely related to the humanistic approach already mentioned, and these terms are sometimes used almost synonymously, together with 'human potential movement', 'sensitivity training' and 'encounter movement'. The general assumption of this movement is that everyone has untapped potential ability for experiencing more fully or satisfyingly or something like that. 'Everyone' seems to mean roughly 'normal adults in Western society'. This potential can be released by various sorts of techniques. No evidence is adduced in support of the assumption, which is in any case stated so variously and so vaguely as almost to defy conceptual analysis. No doubt zealous adherents of the movement count that a virtue.

The techniques turn out to be a bizarre jumble of the supposedly novel and the often ill-understood traditional. Indeed one is tempted to apply to this movement the stricture of H. J. Eysenck on the psychology of Jung: 'What is true in it is not new, and what is new is not true'.

An extensive representative sample of the techniques is given by Lewis and Streitfeld (1972) under the title *Growth Games*. It is quite difficult to know what to make of such collections, whose intentions are, presumably, neither humorous nor cynical. Thus we are advised to achieve 'peak experiences', à la Maslow, by, for example, eating chocolate and listening to Beethoven's Ninth Symphony, while touching fingertips with a person of the opposite sex. The imagination boggles – 'Henry, are you sure this is the *Ninth* Symphony?'

If such tactics can help one person to a richer life, well and good. On the face of it, they seem as far from what I (JR) at least recognize as peaks in my experience (the only one I have for comparison) as a painting by numbers set is from a Rembrandt.

Another 'growth game' is to meditate on a Zen *koan* (see Chapter 5). Even a nodding acquaintance with the literature of Zen ought to have shown that it is not the problem itself that is of any importance, but its use in the whole context of Zen discipline to create the state of 'doubt' without which in Zen, there can be no enlightenment. Mere 'meditation' on such a problem is like putting on your boots in your bedroom and imagining you are climbing Everest.

But enough of such self-styled games, which at best may help the neurotically restricted to a fuller life and at worst seem unworthy of the name 'Psychology'. Psychology as we recognize it has at least struggled, however uncertainly, towards some kind of objectivity and some kind of higher order of understanding.

RK: You have ludicrously distorted the picture by picking on a few weak examples. In preparing for this chapter I examined over 120 such techniques, and could distinguish at least six major groupings: (a) information about oneself; (b) catharsis; (c) bioenergetics; (d) 'mental decomplexing'; (e) relaxation training; (f) meditation/concentration. Each of these really deserves a full analysis.

Perhaps we may see the beginnings of a more productive approach first in the attempt systematically to justify the use of experiential data (e.g. Burt, 1962; Holt, 1964; Radford, 1974); and even more in the application of experimental methods to actual experiences and actual encounters. Prominent in the latter case is the work of Argyle (1967) who in many ingenious investigations has made a start towards showing just how the behaviour of one person directly affects another. For example, just what variables control how closely we approach each other in different situations; for what reasons and with what effect eye contact is maintained; what contributes to or reduces embarrassment in particular cases.

If such analyses can be pursued rigorously and systematically, we might truly become more aware of our own experiences and what controls them, and thus more able to behave realistically and autonomously.

133

One fallacy of too many supposed routes to self-improvement, it seems to me (JR) is the assumption, explicit or implicit, that there exists some kind of ideal natural state in which we are all really free to be ourselves, and that development consists in a return to this paradise. Such a notion goes back, of course, at least to Rousseau (1712–1778) and the myth of the noble savage. This myth may be contrasted with the opposing view of Thomas Hobbes (1588–1679) of the life of primitive man as 'solitary, poor, nasty, brutish, and short'. As far as our knowledge extends, both seem to be caricatures. We have no record of any human group, however lacking in technology, that is without a highly complex social structure. On the other hand such groups are not without their vices and their diseases both physical and mental; and the chances of full individual development, however we conceive this, must be restricted by a subsistence economy and by rigid traditional rules of behaviour. As Delgado (1969) well expresses it, 'liberty is not a natural, inborn characteristic of human expression but a product of awareness and intelligent thinking which must be acquired by conscious individual and collective efforts'. The question arises whether an ideal society can be constructed. Before we discuss it we must at least mention some other issues.

And that is about all we can do. All the important questions remain unanswered. Do the techniques work? Some work in some ways for some people: that is about the best current estimate. Of course it is not clear what we mean by 'work'. We know from many classic studies that if you do almost anything to people, some people will feel better or happier or what not. We might mean that people's self-images can be altered. There is some evidence for this (e.g. Butler and Haigh, 1954) but in itself it tells us little. We might mean that people appear different to others. For this there is less evidence; and still less for what we should really wish to know, whether people actually *behave* differently after some particular process.

Is it possible for everyone to improve, to tap the 'hidden potential' so often talked of? Or are any actual improvements merely the removal of unfortunate handicaps? We do not know.

Do the techniques have anything in common? Since there is as yet no conceptual analysis, it is not really possible to answer. We can suggest, perhaps, that some form of extreme behaviour or feeling is often involved: but even to the most cautious generalization exceptions at once present themselves.

We can also suggest that contrived methods of self-development cannot yet compare with the more fortunate results of ordinary experience. We can, perhaps, improve on nature by conscious effort. It is quite possible to experience extremes of emotion and gain nothing from them. William Blake referred to love as 'continual mutual forgiveness'. It is instructive to compare this with one's own experience, taking it both as a description and an instruction.

Is self-development a matter of withdrawal from life, or acceptance of it? Does it lie in material success or in abnegation? The only answer is 'Yes'. Every conceivable route has been followed with greater or less success. At the simplest level, it is a matter of what one prefers: whether one thinks Christ, or Napoleon, or Bertrand Russell, or Scott of the Antarctic, or Crowley, or Freud, the more admirable character.

At another level, still a pretty simple one, we have suggested that personal growth involves a sense of identity, the ability to act autonomously, and contact with reality. Of course this conceals a host of assumptions. One is that these characteristics are necessarily linked to behaviour we think admirable: respect for others, for example.

135

Another assumption is that there is such a thing as reality, or at the least that we have no choice but to act as if there were. And that to talk (as many mystics have done) of development in terms of 'other realities' is, in the last resort, merely obscurantist.

RK: But to speak of 'other realities' is only 'obscurantist' in the sense that it doesn't currently seem to lead anywhere. It is thus thought to be bogus metaphysics. But, as Kant and others have shown, no metaphysical statement is testable. If it was, it wouldn't be metaphysical. Yet, as Popper and others have demonstrated, a metaphysical statement often leads to a scientific statement, or even becomes one. Our ability to test statements depends upon such factors as apparatus, theories, etc. All of these are changing, and thus a statement about 'other realities' is always potentially a source of scientific advancement. Quite apart from that, there is never science without a metaphysics to support it. Kuhn (1962) has established the need of a scientific community for an unverified set of metaphysical presuppositions to guide their research.

Utopia

Could there be an ideal society? The silly answer is often given that a perfect society would be boring. Silly, because if boredom is a fault, a boring society could not be said to be perfect. The question is whether a society could be constructed so as to increase whatever we think desirable. A utopia would presumably reach some kind of absolute maximum, which seems logically impossible.

There seems little doubt that some past societies have excelled others in the range and variety of their achievements, and almost certainly in our characteristics of self-development. The most often quoted, because the most remarkable, example is that of classical Greece in the sixth and fifth centuries BC. There is no point in trying to summarize the vast literature: for an excellent introduction see *The Greeks* by H. D. F. Kitto (1951). Some important features are these.

First that amazing society was the product of a very complex interaction of factors: geographical, genetic, social, religious, political, etc. Second there was an intense emphasis on individual ability, responsibility, and achievement, and across a whole range of activities. Third, the structure was extremely unstable. Fortunately, weapons more destructive than swords and spears were lacking, but intense rivalry and aggressive independence inevitably led soon to internal collapse and foreign domination.

Thus the Greek achievement, never surpassed and perhaps not equalled – for it was no less than to create science, philosophy, history, and conscious art – seems the result of a happy accident. And so it is with every other great civilization.

Attempts to create deliberately an ideal society have either remained on paper – Plato, More – or if put into practice have fallen far short. Usually, the collapse of communities has been due to lack of size and resources, and/or to the members being largely those who have failed in the larger society outside (see *Utopias and Utopian Thought* by Manuel, 1965).

It is of interest to note one proposed society derived from experimental psychology. In B. F. Skinner's *Walden Two*, everyone is happy and productive due to the beneficent application of operant conditioning (see too B1). Contradictory as this seems, at least one attempt has been made to put it into practice (*Twin Oaks* by Kathleen Kinkade, 1973). The group seems happy enough, but the experimental principles appear more than a little blurred.

On a larger scale such experiments as the Israeli *kibbutzim* have yielded equivocal results (see Wright, 1971). And on a colossal scale, Maoist China presents a picture of (to me, JR) horrifying uniformity.

The social and behavioural sciences can contribute something already to the design of a 'better' society. Taking that knowledge with what else we have from whatever source – history, art, engineering, etc. – it seems we should be able to pick out some factors which *in principle* might be built in to a society such that individual development might be enhanced. It would be essentially a matter of balance: between, for example, authority and freedom; structure and chaos; ritual and spontaneity. Between living close to nature and a civilized artificiality; between an undemanding passivity and a destructive aggression.

My conviction (JR) is that such a society, even if successful, would be inherently unstable. Technological change cannot be permanently halted, and this upsets the delicate balance. The needs of one individual must always in some respects inhibit those of another, and in the long run it is not possible to restrict freedom of choice without thereby losing the liberty which is valuable. Thomas Kuhn (1962) has written of the 'essential tension' – between tradition and innovation – that characterizes highly creative societies. However a state of tension is a state of potential collapse; and so it has always proved.

For my part (JR) I think we might improve our present state by a shift towards the more natural, but also towards the more traditional, ends of some of the spectra. As Paul Goodman (1960) argued, a man who has attained maturity and independence can, perhaps, deal with the chaotic changes of modern society and with luck weld them into a successful way of life. But children, in order to attain such maturity, need a coherent and fairly stable society in which to grow. It seems, at present, impossible to attain the balance.

A. H. Maslow once remarked that if the world is to be saved at all, it will be saved by Psychology. In the end, we agree: but as time goes on, the 'if' gets larger and larger.

138

Selected References and Name Index

The numbers in italics following each entry refer to page numbers within this book

Allport, G. W. (1937; 1961) *Pattern and Growth in Personality.* New York: Holt   *11, 17*

Argyle, M. (1967) *The Psychology of Interpersonal Behaviour.* Harmondsworth: Penguin.   *27, 83, 91*

Aristotle (see Peters, R. S., 1953)   *16, 30, 47, 48, 72*

Bettelheim, B. (1960) *The Informed Heart.* London: Thames and Hudson.   *104*

Delgado, R. (1969) *Physical Control of the Mind.* New York: Harper Colophon.   *98, 134*

Eibl-Eibesfeldt, I. (1970) *Love and Hate.* London: Methuen.   *82*

Eysenck, H. J. (1970) *Crime and Personality.* London: Paladin.   *19, 21, 59, 60, 61, 86, 118, 132*

Freud, S. (1935) *An Autobiographical Study.* London: Hogarth Press.   *11, 15, 22, 29, 30, 42, 53, 54, 62, 68, 69, 72, 73, 80, 88, 90, 114, 121, 122, 125, 128, 130*

Goodman, P. (1961) *Growing Up Absurd.* London: Gollancz.   *40, 138*

James, W. (1902) *The Varieties of Religious Experience.* London: Longmans.   *27, 65, 66, 77, 78*

Jung, C. G. (1963) *Memories, Dreams, Reflections*. London: Fontana. *60, 62, 73, 113, 121, 122, 132*

Kitto, H. D. F. (1951) *The Greeks*. Harmondsworth: Penguin. *137*

Kuhn, T. S. (1962) *The Structure of Scientific Revelations*. Chicago University Press. *138*

Lazarus, R. and Opton, E. M. (1967) *Personality*. Harmondsworth: Penguin. *85*

Lewis, H. R. and Streitfeld, H. S. (1972) *Growth Games*. London: Souvenir Press/Sphere Books. *132*

Lifton, R. J. (1963) *Thought Reform and the Psychology of Totalism*. New York: Norton. *105*

Madsen, K. B. (1961) *Theories of Motivation*. Copenhagen: Munksgaard. *58*

Maslow, A. (1962) *Toward a Psychology of Being*. London: Van Nostrand. *119, 120, 128, 138*

Peters, R. S. (1953) *Brett's History of Psychology*. London: Allen and Unwin.

Peters, R. S. (1958) *The Concept of Motivation*. London: Routledge and Kegan Paul. *14, 54, 56, 57, 67, 68, 69*

Popper, K. (1963) *Conjectures and Refutations*. London: Routledge and Kegan Paul. *12, 15, 16, 41, 43*

Radford, J. and Burton, A. (1974) *Thinking: Its Nature and Development*. London: Wiley. *18, 125, 133*

Ruddock, R. (1972) *Six Approaches to the Person*. London: Routledge and Kegan Paul. *11*

Strongman, K. (1973) *The Psychology of Emotion*. London: Wiley. *79*

Subject Index